Who can know the mind of God…?
But we have the mind of Christ.

—Paul, 1 Cor 2:16

The Mind of Christ:

The Truth About Jesus

David & Retta Thayer

This book was prepared with Microsoft® Publisher 2010 running on 64-bit Microsoft Windows® 7 Professional. PDF output through Adobe® Acrobat® X.

Printed on 60-pound acid-free archival paper for longevity.
Manufactured in the United States of America

Published by the Universal Christ Church Press
An imprint of Rapidsoft Press®   SAN 299-5840
Sarasota, Florida

ISBN 978-0-9663909-6-4
First edition, second printing

To Richard M. Bucke: You were the first to understand.

In Memoriam

Retta M. Thayer, 1937–2011

Retta Thayer, the junior author of this work, passed away somewhat unexpectedly on August 5, 2011, leaving this work in an unfinished state. The remaining work on the manuscript was done by the senior author, David Thayer. Retta was a highly spiritual individual, and although she is sorely missed, she is now with her Lord and needs nothing further from this ephemeral world—a world whose true nature she knew intimately from her many studies, not the least of which was the work she did on this manuscript.

Preface

IT IS VIRTUALLY CERTAIN THAT MORE BOOKS have been written about one man from Nazareth than about any other person in history. It is nearly as certain that not one of them has tried to describe the particular nature of the consciousness of that man. In his book *The Consciousness of Jesus*, Jacques Guillet writes:

> Without embarking on such a chimeric adventure as exploring Jesus' consciousness and reconstructing his spiritual itinerary, and without seeking to know what the texts do not tell us, it is not illusory to try to rediscover, in the texts themselves, the presence and the action of Jesus' consciousness.

Yet it is precisely "such a chimeric adventure" that is required if we are to discover who and what Jesus really was. Guillet does not make the attempt, nor does William Barclay in his book, *The Mind of Jesus*. It may well be that on some library shelf there is a book about Jesus that does attempt to describe his consciousness. If so, neither of us is aware of its existence.

In days gone by it was sufficient to say that Jesus was the Son of God, God and man made one. Today, in the twenty-first century with the threat of thermonuclear war still clouding our tomorrows, we live in a world populated by quarks, quasars, and gluons. In our time rockets carry men to the moon and robot laboratories to Venus and Mars; scientists grow human babies in petri dishes and grope for the secrets of the genetic code; giant telescopes show us images of unimaginably distant galaxies as they were fourteen billion years ago; and surgeons almost routinely disconnect a patient's heart in order to repair it. With the vastly expanded world view we have today, the old answers—which only beg more questions—are simply not good enough.

The men and women of today want concrete answers to their questions in terms they can understand. And who can blame them? There are such answers to millions of other questions. Our question is: What was the nature of the consciousness of Jesus of Nazareth? Should there not be a solid, understandable, even scientific answer to this question?

For all of you who would like to have such an answer we have good news: The answer is in this book, although it is not original here. There already is a book that attempts to describe the consciousness of Jesus, but it is not a book about Jesus. Rather it is a book about all of those persons, living at different times and in different places, who apparently received the same peculiar sort of consciousness that Jesus so eminently possessed. The person who discovered them was Richard Maurice Bucke, a Canadian physician. In his youth Bucke enjoyed, for a few fleeting moments, the same kind of consciousness. The experience so changed him that for the rest of his life he spent as much time as he could looking for reports from others who might have had a similar experience. His search was amply rewarded. The result was a book published in 1900 with the title *Cosmic Consciousness: A Study in the Evolution of the Human Mind*. William James, author of *The Varieties of Religious Experience*, wrote:

> I believe that you have brought this kind of consciousness 'home' to the attention of students of human nature in a way so definite and inescapable that it will be impossible henceforward to overlook or ignore it. . . . you are a benefactor of us all.

Unfortunately, William James was wrong. In the years since—to the profound discredit of the human race—Bucke has been almost universally ignored. Our purpose in this book is to change that implicit verdict by presenting the evidence in favor of Bucke's hypothesis in such strong and cogent terms that it will forever more be impossible to ignore.

We have been helped in this task by the many changes that have occurred since 1900 in those factors that must strongly influence any study of the historical Jesus. The advent of "form criticism" has profoundly changed the prevailing viewpoint on the authenticity and significance of textual source materials, whether these be the canonical gospels or the so-called apocryphal writings. Many of these changes tend to support Bucke's hypothesis at the expense of more orthodox theological interpretations. Discoveries of ancient manuscripts, such as the Dead Sea Scrolls and the Nag Hammadi library, have added greatly to the available source materials. And last, but far from least, the ready availability of high-speed information processing techniques made possible by the micro-computer revolution has given us a powerful new tool for the analysis of textual correlations. We have tried to make maximum use of these new tools and resources to make this study of the mind of Christ as thorough and unbiased as possible. You, the reader, will be the ultimate judge of how successful we have been.

BUT WE DARE NOT CLOSE HERE WITHOUT A WARNING. This book is difficult, perhaps dangerous. If you already have faith in Christ you may find many of the concepts presented here shocking or even blasphemous. At the least, some of your most cherished beliefs will be challenged. Nevertheless, you should press on. If you feel uncomfortable—even afraid—then you are one of those to whom this book is especially directed. The more you feel threatened by the book, the more you should be determined to finish it. Once you really begin to understand it, it will become much easier. You may find a reconciliation before you reach the end.

In any event, the only correct way to read this book is with a deliberate suspension of judgment until you have finished it. Then, when you have all the facts at your disposal, the choice is yours. But be aware, before you start, that this book serves a dual purpose: It is both an informative text and a Teaching Story, like *Seven Arrows*. When you have finished, you should know enough to make your choice wisely, with full awareness of the possible consequences.

David & Retta Thayer
Salem, Oregon, 1996

Introduction

BEFORE WE WADE INTO the deep waters to come, there are a few formalities we must dispose of. These concern some details of the terminology we shall be using.

Dates

First of all, there is the matter of dates. Throughout this book we shall use the symbols BC and AD to refer to dates. Notice that there are no periods in these; they are presented as if they were acronyms, although they are not. We use them in place of the awkward B.C.E. and C.E. used by most authors these days. These stand for "Before Common Era" and "Common Era," respectively. They correspond, in fact, to the more usual B.C. ("Before Christ") and A.D. ("*Anno Domini*" meaning "Year of Our Lord"). Most authors do not wish to use B.C. and A.D. because of their religious connotations, so they use B.C.E. and C.E. There is, however, nothing "common" about the A.D./ C.E. era. Many peoples use dates based on entirely different eras— Jews and Muslims for instance. If the "C" stood for "Current" these two abbreviations might make more sense. In any event, most people are accustomed to seeing the terms B.C. and A.D. used for dates. We drop the periods from these to emphasize that they do not stand for the religious terms normally denoted, but are used merely as a convenient notation. With this conversion we point out that the date 1992 AD is correct, whereas 1992 A.D. is incorrect (it should be written as A.D. 1992). Moreover, BC and AD are more compact than B.C.E. and C.E.

The name of Jesus:

The mistransliteration of a Greek mistransliteration

Yeshua is the original Aramaic proper name for Jesus the Nazarene, who lived from about 2 BC to 30 AD. The word "Jesus" is actually a mistransliteration of a Greek mistransliteration. The Emperor Constantine even mistook Jesus for Apollo, the son of the Greek god Zeus.

Yeshua Ben Yosef

It is most proper to call him Yeshua. It was indeed his proper name, given to him by his parents, and only in Hebrew does this name have any meaning. In Hebrew Yeshua means both "Salvation," and the concatenated form of Yahoshua, is "Lord who is Salvation." The name Jesus has no intrinsic meaning in English whatsoever.

There are many Yeshuas that we read about in Biblical text and many are confused with the Yeshua who would later become the "Christ." The name Yeshua appears 29 times in the Tanach. Yehoshua (Joshua) of Nun is called Yeshua in Nechemyah (Nehemiah) 8:17. Yeshua is the name of the Cohain HaGadol (the high priest) in the time of Zerubavel in Ezra 3:2. It is the name of a Levite under King Hezekiah in 2 Chronicles 31:15. There is even a city called Yeshua in the Negev of Yehudah in Nechemyah 11:26. Yeshua is also a shortened version of the name Yehoshua much like Bill is for William.

There are 7 other Yeshua's (Jesuses) in the Brit Chadashah. There is Elymas bar Yeshua in Acts 13:6. There is an ancestor of Yeshua, HaMashiach: the son of Eliezar, the father of Er in Luke 3:29. In Rav Shaul's letter to the Colossians in chapter 4, verse 11, there is a Justus called Yeshua, a fellow worker of Saul. Josephus, the famous Jewish historian mentions 20 different Yeshua's (Jesuses), ten of which are contemporary with Yeshua HaMashiach. Altogether, at least 50

Yeshuas from his time plus about nine in the Tanach have been revealed from Biblical texts and other literary sources.

Mistranslating the Mistranslation

Yeshua is a Hebrew name which has been transliterated into Greek as Iesous (IhsouV: pronounced "ee-ay-SUS"). The English "Jesus" comes from the Latin transliteration of the Greek name into the Latin Jesus. Now Greek has no "y" sound, but the Latin "i" is both an "i" and a "j" (i.e., it can have a consonantal force in front of other vowels), the latter of which is properly pronounced like the English "y" (which explains the German Jesu, "YAY-su") That is why we spell Jesus as we do, taking it straight from Latin, but we pronounce the name with a soft "j" sound because that is what we do in English with the consonantal "j."

The first letter in the name Yeshua ("Jesus") is the yod. Yod represents the "Y" sound in Hebrew. Many names in the Bible that begin with yod are mispronounced by English speakers because the yod in these names was transliterated in English Bibles with the letter "J" rather than "Y." This came about because in early English the letter "J" was pronounced the way we pronounce "Y" today. All proper names in the Old Testament were transliterated into English according to their Hebrew pronunciation via the Latin, but when English pronunciation shifted to what we know today, these transliterations were not altered. Thus, such Hebrew place names as ye-ru-sha-LA-yim, ye-ri-HO, and yar-DEN have become known to us as Jerusalem, Jericho, and Jordan; and Hebrew personal names such as yo-NA, yi-SHAI, and ye-SHU-a have become known to us as Jonah, Jesse, and Jesus. To further complicate matters, there was no letter "J" in the old English alphabet and the letter "I" was often used in its place. Often in early texts of the time, Jesus or Jerusalem would be spelled Iesus or Ierusalem.

The second sound in Yeshua's name is called tse-RE, and is pronounced almost like the letter "e" in the word "net." Just as the "Y" sound of the first letter is mispronounced in today's English, so too the first vowel sound in "Jesus." Before the Hebrew name "Yeshua" was transliterated into English, it was first transliterated into Greek. There was no difficulty in transliterating the tse-RE sound since the ancient Greek language had an equivalent letter which represented this sound. And there was no real difficulty in transcribing this same first vowel into English. The translators of the earliest versions of the English Bible transliterated the tse-RE in Yeshua with an "e." Unfortunately, later English speakers guessed wrongly that this "e" should be pronounced as in "me," and thus the first syllable of the English version of Yeshua came to be pronounced "Jee" instead of "Yeh." It is this pronunciation that produced such euphemistic profanities as "Gee" and "Geez."

Since Yeshua is spelled "Jeshua" and not "Jesus" in most English versions of the Old Testament (for example in Ezra 2:2 and 2 Chronicles 31:15), one easily gets the impression that the name is never mentioned in the Hebrew Scriptures. Yet "Yeshua" appears there twenty-nine times, and is the name of at least five different persons and one village in the southern part of Yehudah ("Judah").

In contrast to the early biblical period, there were relatively few different names in use among the Jewish population of the Land of Israel at the time of the Second Temple. The name Yeshua was one of the most common male names in that period, tied with Eleazer for fifth place behind Simon, Joseph, Judah, and John. Nearly one out of ten persons known from the period was named Yeshua.

The first sound of the second syllable of Yeshua is the "sh" sound. It is represented by the Hebrew letter shin. However Greek, like many other languages, has no "sh" sound. Instead, the closest approximation, the Greek sigma, was used when transcribing "Yeshua" as "Iesus." Translators of English versions of the New Testament transliterated the Greek transcription of a Hebrew name, instead of returning to the original Hebrew. This was doubly unfortunate, first because the "sh" sound exists in English, and second because in English the "s" sound can shift to the "z" sound, which is what happened in the case of the pronunciation of "Jesus."

The fourth sound one hears in the name Yeshua is the "u" sound, as in the word "true". Like the first three sounds, this also has come to be mispronounced but in this case it is not the fault of the translators. They transcribed this sound accurately, but English is not a phonetic language and "u" can be pronounced in more than one way. At some point the "u" in "Jesus" came to be pronounced as in "cut," and so we say "Jee-zuhs."

The "a" sound, as in the word "father," is the fifth sound in Jesus's name. It is followed by a guttural produced by contracting the lower throat muscles and retracting the tongue root—an unfamiliar task for English speakers. In an exception to the rule, the vowel sound "a" associated with the last letter "ayin" (the guttural) is pronounced before it, not after. While there is no equivalent in English or any other Indo-European language, it is somewhat similar to the last sound in the name of the composer, "Bach." In this position it is almost inaudible to the western ear. Some Israelis pronounce this last sound and some don't, depending on what part of the Diaspora their families returned from. The Hebrew Language Academy, guardian of the purity of the language, has ruled that it should be sounded, and Israeli radio and television announcers are required to pronounce it correctly. There was no letter to represent them, and so these fifth and sixth sounds were dropped from the Greek transcription of "Yeshua"—the transcription from which the English "Jesus" is derived.

So where did the final "s" of "Jesus" come from? Masculine names in Greek ordinarily end with a consonant, usually with an "s" sound, and less frequently with an "n" or "r" sound. In the case of "Iesus," the Greeks added a sigma, the "s" sound, to close the word. The same is true for the names Nicodemus, Judas, Lazarus, and others.

English speakers make one final change from the original pronunciation of Jesus's name. English places the accent on "Je," rather than on "sus." Thus, the "u" has been shortened in its English pronunciation to "uh."

In Yeshua's Name

Today's tradition of pronouncing his completely Hellenized name as "Jesus" has indeed obscured his true name, "Yeshua," and has shifted its perceived meaning much like most of his original teachings.

Even his name, it would seem, became a part of this understand-ing. The name Jesus or Jesus Christ is often used in everything from idle conversation, to bumper stickers and jewelry, to enforcing false teachings, to justifying wars and political agendas, and is even used as a profanity. The name Yeshua however, has remained pure and holy, known and used only by those who would uphold His name and teachings in the highest regard and thus reserving his holy name for use only in spiritual matters and the most humbled and sincere of prayer and obeisance.

This section is from a web page of "Yis'rael the Nation of YHWH" at:

http://israelseed.tripod.com/id24.html

discovered by one of the authors (Retta) in 2008.

The land where Yeshua lived

Now we pass on to the name of the land where Jesus lived and died. In most texts you will see this land referred to as Palestine. Jesus did not live in Palestine. There was no such place then. The name Palestine was applied to the land in 135 AD by the Roman emperor Hadrian. Because the Jews had shown the unmitigated gall to rebel against mighty Rome not just once but twice, Hadrian in effect kicked them out of their own land and renamed it *Syria Palaestina*, which has evolved into the modern name Palestine. Imperial Rome was probably the most ruthless aggressor and colonial power in the history of the world. They had no more right to rename Judea than Japan did to rename Korea as "Chosen" in the 1930s. The name Palestine is therefore illegitimate. If we are going to use anachronistic names for places, then we should use the latest, most legitimate name available. That name is Israel, the name given to the land by the Jews, who have the oldest claim to it (their claim goes back some 3,000 years, whereas that of the so-called Palestinians goes back only about 1,200 years). We shall refer to the land as it was called in the time of Jesus. Most of his life was spent in Galilee, although he also went into Judea and Samaria. You will not see the illegitimate name Palestine again in this book.

Terminology

There are also a number of technical terms we shall be using throughout this book that need definitions for those readers who are not familiar with biblical research terminology. We could probably have written this book without using any of these terms, but they are so convenient to use—which is precisely why they were invented in the first place—that we decided to use them anyway. These terms and their definitions follow. Please take the time to read through these and understand their meanings. You will encounter them frequently throughout this book.

Christology. A theological interpretation of the person and work of Christ, often doctrinal. Especially, a theory or doctrine of how Yeshua came to be the Messiah, or Christ. The current Christology of the Christian church is that Yeshua was born of the virgin Mary, fully man and fully God, and represents the second person of the Trinity. The Roman Catholic Christology goes one step further, holding that Mary was herself the product of an "Immaculate Conception," and thus also was free of Original Sin. As we shall see, there were various other Christologies that saw their day in the early church, some of them much older and more original than these. We call ours "the rebirth Christology."

Church Fathers. The authoritative early writers of the Christian church who established doctrines and set standards for religious rites and ceremonies.

Circa. Usually abbreviated "ca," means "on or about" the given date(s).

Eschatology. Religious doctrines concerning last or final matters, such as death, judgment, or afterlife.

Israel. Used here to denote the land comprising the provinces of Judea, Samaria, and Galilee during the time of Yeshua.

Kerygma. The preaching or proclamation of the gospel, particularly in the early church. Also, the gospel as preached by the Apostles. Used in biblical research to refer to the core beliefs of the early church as embodied in its teachings.

Passion. The sufferings of Christ on the cross or subsequent to the Last Supper; the narrative of Christ's sufferings. Extended by many authors to include the Resurrection as well.

Pericope. Literally, an excerpt from or section of a text. Used in biblical text criticism to indicate a section of text that forms a logical whole. The gospels are typically composed of pericopes, presumably obtained from oral tradition, that have been linked together with short sections of transitional text that serve to set the scene for the next pericope.

Proof-text. A section of text from the so-called Old Testament quoted in support of a point made in the New Testament, or text from the Old Testament used as a part of the New Testament, both to show continuity between the two texts and to invoke the Old Testament's power of prophecy in support of New Testament writings.

RSV. The Revised Standard Version of the Bible.

Synoptic gospels. The first three gospels (Mark, Matthew, Luke—in chronological order) are called "synoptic" (taking the same viewpoint) because they are arranged in the same order and agree with one another in many major respects.

Yeshua. This is the true name of the man called Jesus in Bibles (see previous section). We shall not use the name "Jesus" in this book. All references will be to either Yeshua or Yeshu (a diminutive). According to the author of "Jesus or Yeshua" (see previous section "The name of Jesus"), the name Yeshua is itself a diminutive of the name Yeshoshua, usually rendered in English as "Joshua." With some exceptions—mostly book titles—you have seen the last of the misnomer "Jesus" right here.

～ ✺ ～

Table of Contents

The Mind of Christ

Chapter 1
The Wellspring: Sources & Methods

WHERE DID WE GET OUR INFORMATION AND HOW DID WE USE IT? These are important questions if we are to understand someone who lived two millennia ago and about whom a large body of mythology and not a little bit of disinformation has accrued. First, we shall describe the sources of our information: the ancient texts concerning Christ and his followers. Then we shall explore the methods we and others have used to distill some truth from a remarkable accumulation of frequently contradictory evidence.

The ancient texts

We shall use both canonical (accepted by the church for inclusion in the bible) and non-canonical sources in our investigation. The primary sources we used are listed here in approximately the order in which they were written—approximate because for none of them is the date definitely known.

Letters of Paul, Gospels, and other canonical scriptures

The Letters of Paul are believed to have been written before any of the Gospels, either canonical or non-canonical (we avoid the use of the term "apocryphal," which is often used for non-canonical texts because it implies that they are not genuine; this is no longer believed to be true and they are widely used by authors to compare with canonical scriptures). Because of what Paul knew when he wrote these letters, and even more importantly, the things he did not know of, his letters are dated to approximately 50 to 60 AD. The most significant of these letters we use here are the two letters to the Corinthians, Galatians, Romans, and Hebrews, which has been attributed to Paul but is likely by some unknown author.

The books of the canonical New Testament are now believed to have been written in the following order, which is after Marcus J. Borg (2012). Most of Paul's letters and similar texts are at the beginning of this list and are some of our earliest sources for material about Yeshua.

1. First Thessalonians, a letter of Paul written about 48–50 AD.
2. Galatians, another letter of Paul written about 50–52 AD.
3. First Corinthians, a letter of Paul written ca 52 AD.
4. Philemon, a letter of Paul written ca 52–54 AD, while he was in a Roman prison.
5. Philippians, another letter of Paul written from prison, probably in Ephesus, ca 54–55 AD.
6. Second Corinthians, three letters of Paul combined into one, written ca 56 AD.
7. Romans, the last letter of Paul, written in Corinth ca 58 AD.
8. Mark, the earliest Gospel, written ca 70 AD, possibly in Galilee.
9. James, written by an unknown author probably between 60 and 80 AD.
10. Colossians, by another unknown author, probably written in the early 80s AD.
11. Matthew, the second Gospel, which was written in the 80s or early 90s AD.

12. Hebrews, an important text by an unknown author, written ca 85 AD.
13. John, the third Gospel, written ca 90–95 AD.
14. Ephesians, another text attributed wrongly to Paul, written ca 90 AD.
15. Revelation, the last book in the Christian bible, probably written in the mid 90s AD.
16. Jude, another work by an unknown author, dated ca 100 AD.
17. First, Second, and Third John, probably written by the same author ca 100 AD.
18. Luke, the fourth Gospel, written ca 110 AD, although a date as early as 80 AD is not impossible.
19. Acts, written by the author of Luke, probably at the same time, ca 100–120 AD.
20. Second Thessalonians, believed written by someone other than Paul ca 95–110 AD.
21. First Peter, not written by Peter but in his name, probably in the early second century AD.
22. First and Second Timothy, written in Paul's name but not by him, ca 110-130 AD.
23. Titus, written by an unknown author ca 110-130 AD.
24. Second Peter, written by an unknown author ca 120-150 AD.

Altogether there are twenty-seven canonical New Testament texts. The term "canonical" means that they were made officially a part of the Christian canon. The decision was made by church authorities during the second through fourth centuries AD, most likely because these texts agreed with the current Christian dogma. This fixing of the New Testament scriptures was not done at the Council of Nicaea (325 AD), despite common belief.

IN ADDITION to the canonical texts there are many non-canonical texts, some of which are gospels in their own right and others of which are logia (collections of saying). Some of them are fragmentary. The most important of these documents and their approximate dates of composition are as follows:

1. The *Gospel of Thomas*, a collection of sayings attributed to Yeshua, found at Nag Hammadi, Egypt, in 1945. We shall refer to this one often. The Coptic Thomas found at Nag Hammadi dates to ca 340 AD. Other documents in Greek found at Oxyrhynchus, Egypt, before 1945 were found to be parts of the Coptic *Thomas*; these papyrus fragments date to between 130 and 250 AD.

2. The *Gospel of Mary*, a fragmentary text about Miriam of Magdala (Mary Magdalene) was discovered first in 1896 but only fragments of the papyrus document remain. It was written in the early second century AD and presents Christianity in a completely different light than the canonical texts. The principal story of the remaining document is that of a conflict between Miriam and Peter, the apostle, which is then resolved by Levi (possibly the apostle Matthew).

3. The *Didache* or *Teaching of the Twelve Apostles*, a document lost for centuries but found as a Greek text in 1873, and in a Latin version in 1900. It dates to the last half of the first century AD.

4. The *Epistle of Barnabas*, called by the biblical scholar Geza Vermes as "the earliest work of gentile Christianity," dates to between 70 AD and 135 AD; Vermes postulates 120 AD as the most likely date.

5. The *Acts of Paul and Thecla*, another non-canonical work, dates to the second century AD. It contains the only known physical description of the apostle Paul.

Although we may refer to other non-canonical texts, these five are probably the most important to our case.

Also, there are a number of reference works that were very important in making our case for the nature of Yeshua's consciousness. Chief among them are the following:

1. *The Interpreter's Bible*. Twelve volumes. Nashville, Tennessee: Abingdon Press, 1957 and later editions.

2. *Modern Concordance to the New Testament*. Michael Darton, ed. Garden City, New York: Doubleday & Company, 1976.

3.   *Jesus of Nazareth*. Joseph Klausner. New York: The Macmillan Company, 1946.
4.   *The Quest of the Historical Jesus*. Albert Schweitzer. New York: The Macmillan Company, 1968.
5.   *The Mysticism of Paul the Apostle*. Albert Schweitzer. New York: The Seabury Press, 1968.
6.   *Rabbi Jesus: An Intimate Biography*. Bruce Chilton. New York: Doubleday (Random House), 2002.

The task of theology

No matter how carefully they may seek to avoid doing so, theologians must inevitably deal with the problem that God, as the Creator, is ultimately responsible for the condition of the world. We may not duck this issue with the lame assertion that it is man, not God, who has messed things up. We cannot assume that the world and mankind are somehow separate from God, things for which He is not responsible. No, if God is to be thought of as "a Being than which no greater can be imagined," then the universe—and mankind—must be somehow part of God. If this were not so, then the union of God and the universe would comprise something greater than God—an absurd conclusion.[†]

This brings us up sharply against the problem of evil, a problem that has confounded the best efforts of theologians for centuries. How can evil exist in a world created by a loving God? How are we to account for all the pain and suffering that occurs in our world?

If we start from scratch with the concept that a loving, all-powerful God creates this world and its inhabitants, we must

---

[†] The term "union" comes from mathematical set theory. A "set" is a collection of objects. The union of two sets contains all of the objects in both sets. If the "set of all sets" be defined as U, then the union of U and any set is impossible, because by definition, U already contains "any set." Therefore, God, as U, must contain the universe, since the universe is by definition a set. If the universe is not part of God, then the union of God and the universe would be greater than God, which is impossible if God is U—by definition: "a Being than which no greater can be imagined."

assume that this world is, therefore, the best of all possible worlds. It is best from God's standpoint, however, not necessarily from ours. In other words, this world is created to serve perfectly God's purposes in creating it. From our limited human viewpoint it may well be one of the worst of conceivable worlds. Any theology must show that this world serves God's purpose in creating it, and in the process of so doing explain the existence of evil. A theology that does not do this is not worth the paper it is printed on. We state here categorically that the theory we shall present in this book does so, and does so decisively.

This is not the place to describe this theology. It will become apparent as our analysis of Yeshua of Nazareth unfolds. Here we merely wish to point out the source of the error that has prevented this theology from being discovered previously: ultimate ego-centricity. The original egocentric error was the belief that our planet comprised the universe. When it was discovered that there were stars and planets exterior to our world, the error shifted to the belief that our planet was the center of the universe. Later, the error shifted to the belief that our sun was the center of the universe. Today even that belief has fallen by the wayside. Yet the egocentric error remains, so well hidden that few suspect its existence. The ultimate egocentric error is the belief that our universe is the center of existence, the primary vessel for life. Anyone who believes the teachings of Christ should know that this is patently false, yet today virtually everyone subscribes to it. But to be a follower of Christ one must relinquish this belief. It is false theology.

Theological criteria for the study of Yeshua

There are probably as many theories about Yeshua as there are books about him. The authors of these theories have invariably sought to support their arguments by quoting sayings of Yeshua, and sections of the gospels, that appear to agree with their theories. However, selecting portions of the texts in support of an argument is an invalid criterion for demonstrating the truth of the argument. It has been truly said that almost anything can be 'proved' by judicious selection

of Biblical passages. We propose here the use of a much more rigor-
ous criterion: comparison of the argument with *all of the relevant
texts*. For a study of the consciousness of Yeshua, these texts
comprise the four gospels, Mark, Matthew, Luke, and John, as well
as portions of Acts, the letters of Paul, and certain 'apocryphal'
writings, principally the so-called Gospel of Thomas (which is really
a collection of logia, or sayings) and the surviving fragments of the
Gospel of Mary.

The relative degree of success of a given theory is measured,
under this criterion, by the ratio of the number of textual pericopes
that are consistent with the hypothesis to the total number of
pericopes in the texts. Because of the uncertain authenticity of some
of the pericopes, no hard figure can be given for the percentage of
successful matches that must be attained before a particular theory
can be considered valid. The most successful theory to date is the
orthodox Christian interpretation of Yeshua, but even this theology
has problems with certain of the texts. For example, the saying of
Yeshua "The wind blows where it wills, and you hear the sound of it,
but you do not know whence it comes or whither it goes; so it is
with every one who is born of the spirit" [Jn 3:8] is difficult to
interpret within orthodox Christian theology. Even more trouble-
some is Yeshua's cry from the cross "My God, my God, why have
You forsaken me?" [Mk 15:34] Yeshua's saying "Why do you call me
good? Only God is good" [Mk 10:18; Lk 18:19] poses even worse
difficulties. And today many theologians find it hard to believe that
Yeshua really said ". . . no one comes to the Father, but by me."
[Jn 14:6; cf. Weatherhead, Leslie D., *The Christian Agnostic*, p. 66.]
(Nevertheless, as we shall see, the saying *is* true.) Be all this as it
may, we state here unequivocally that the theory of Yeshua presented in this book is consistent with every part of the texts against
which it can be compared—including those above, which are so
difficult from the standpoint of orthodox Christianity.

The principle of potential exclusion

One of the most potent of the criteria for judging the accuracy of
reported sayings of Yeshua is what we like to call "the principal of

potential exclusion." Put simply, the more a statement of Yeshua deviates from the beliefs of the church, the more likely it is to have been excised, or redacted, from a scriptural text. Take, for an example, the saying "Why do you call me good? Only God is good" mentioned above. The foundation belief of the church is that Yeshua was the second person of the Trinity, the Son of God. How then could he have said the words written in Mark 10:18 and Luke 18:19? These words are in direct opposition to the beliefs of the church. Their survival in these extant Gospels is almost a guarantee that they are genuine. If there had been the slightest doubt that they were not a true saying of Yeshua, they surely would have been redacted from the Gospels of Mark and Luke.

By the same token, the more a saying attributed to Yeshua agrees with the current beliefs of the church, the more suspicious it becomes. For example, the disciple Peter (Cephas) could not possibly have told Yeshua in Matthew 16:16: "You are the Christ, the Son of the living God," because "Christ" is a Greek word and Peter was speaking Aramaic, and the idea that Christ was the Son of God had not even been conceived of then. What he undoubtedly did say was "You are the Messiah" (compare with Mark 8:29). The words as reported in Matthew were invented by the church long after Yeshua was gone. We shall return to this point later.

The Shroud of Turin

The only possible picture we have of Yeshua is the image on the so-called Shroud of Turin. As you may know, this linen shroud appeared in history about the 14TH century. It is believed by many to be the actual burial cloth of Yeshua bearing the "miraculous" imprint of the crucified Yeshua. It is essentially a photographic negative, a fact that was discovered in 1898

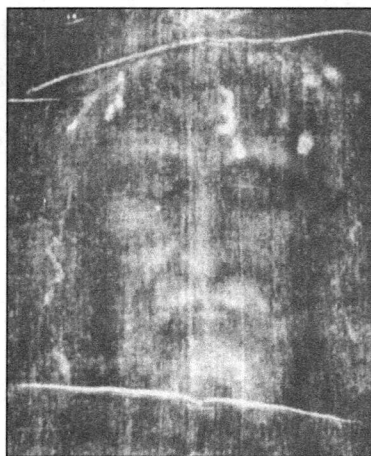

Face of the man on the Shroud

when an amateur Italian photographer, Secondo Pia, was allowed to photograph the shroud in the Turin cathedral. Upon examining his negative plate, Pia was amazed to see that it appeared to be a positive image. Pia was at first accused of doctoring his photographs, but was vindicated in 1931 when professional photographer Giuseppe Enrie photographed the shroud and his findings supported those of Pia. (*Wikipedia*).

After a digital study in 1978, NASA researchers Jackson, Jumper, and Stephenson reported detecting the impressions of coins placed on both eyes (it was customary in those days to place coins over the eyes of the deceased). The two-lepton coin on the right eyelid was presumably coined under Pilatus in 29–30, while the one-lepton coin on the left eyelid was minted in 29 AD. The authenticity of these alleged coins is in dispute at the time of this writing (2014); but evidence that they are genuine appears strong. (*Wikipedia, Williams*)

The mystery of the Shroud

The 1988 carbon-14 dating of the Shroud of Turin only deepens the mystery posed by this ancient relic. Some evidence exists suggesting that the dating is incorrect; allegedly, the tests may have been deliberately manipulated so as to produce a date in the 14TH century. Recent articles have stated that carbon-14 dating of cloth samples so old as that is intrinsically inaccurate. But even if the dating is correct, it raises far more questions than it answers. To begin with, it seems impossible that the Shroud could have been forged by a 14TH-century person. The reasons for this are numerous, but consist chiefly of the following:

❑ The image on the Shroud is a perfect photographic nega-tive. The first time that anyone saw the positive image was after photographs were taken of the Shroud in the late 19TH century. No one in the 14TH century could possibly have known how to produce a photographic negative image. And no modern artist has been able to duplicate the image on the Shroud, even after its nature as a negative image had been revealed.

❑ The man on the Shroud is naked. In the 14ᵀᴴ century it would have been horribly sacreligious for anyone to have depicted Yeshua in the nude.

❑ The wounds from the nails are in the wrists. No one in the 14ᵀᴴ century knew that this was the way crucifixions were done, although we now know this to have been the case. In any event, the wounds in the crucified Yeshua were always shown in the palms of the hands. For a forger to have done otherwise would have been to invite disbelief.

❑ The wounds from the crown of thorns show that it was actually a cap, rather than a ring. But all other 14ᵀᴴ-century depictions show the crown of thorns as a ring around his head. To have shown it as having been a cap rather than a ring would have been to invite still further disbelief.

❑ The abrasions produced when the condemned man carried his cross to the place of execution show that it was only the horizontal cross-piece (the *patibulum*) that was carried. All other 14ᵀᴴ-century depictions show Yeshua carrying the complete cross. Again, to have shown otherwise would have been to invite disbelief. No competent forger—and if the Shroud is a forgery, its maker was nothing if not competent—working in the 14ᵀᴴ century would conceivably have committed the series of blunders comprising this and the three previous points.

❑ A relic later called "The Mandylion" was recovered in the 6ᵀᴴ century in Edessa (now in Turkey). At that time artists' representations of the face of Yeshua changed radically and became similar to the face of the Man of the Shroud. It seems very likely that the Shroud was the relic known as the Mandylion, in which case it could not have been made in the 14ᵀᴴ century.

If the Shroud really was produced in the 14ᵀᴴ century, as the carbon-14 dating seems to indicate, then the first five of these considerations suggest that there was only one person with both the knowledge and the ability to have produced it: God Himself.

And that's more of a mystery than the Shroud itself.

A possible solution that may have been overlooked

Here is a possibility that no one seems to have thought of. Suppose that the original Shroud was genuine and that it was copied by an extremely proficient forger in the 14TH century. The copy survived as the present Shroud of Turin, but the original was somehow lost in the Middle Ages. Let us compare the implications of this conjecture with the facts at hand.

Picknett (*The Turin Shroud: How Da Vinci Fooled History* by Lynn Picknett and Clive Price, New York: Simon and Schuster, 2007) suggests that perhaps Leonardo Da Vinci forged the Shroud. Certainly an artist of Da Vinci's stature would have been required to have done this, since no modern artist (or scientist) has been able to make a comparable copy of the Shroud.

This theory explains at one stroke the objections listed above against the Shroud having been a forgery. The forger—or perhaps "copyist" would be a better term here—must have been convinced beyond any reasonable doubt that the shroud he was copying was genuine, as otherwise he would not have made the apparently incredible blunders in the above list (the second through fifth points). The first point is negated since the copyist would have been copying (albeit unknowingly) what later turned out to have been a photographic negative. The final point concerning the Mandylion is rendered moot, regardless of its truth or falsity.

The Shroud of Turin in positive and negative views

The picture on the next page shows photographs of the Shroud of Turin, printed first (on the left) directly from the photographic negative, and second (on the right) as a direct positive print. The positive print is how the Shroud would appear were you to view it yourself. The negative image on the left shows the true nature of the picture on the Shroud as a negative image, since making a negative of a negative image creates a positive image. Not until the first photograph was made of the Shroud in 1898 was the true nature of the image on the Shroud revealed.

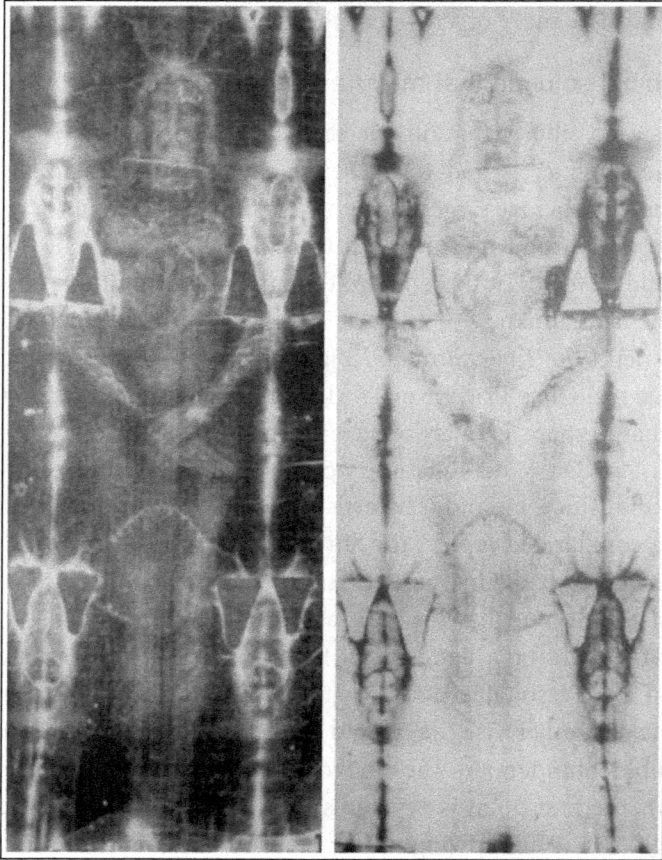

The Shroud of Turin: Positive and Negative Views

The image on the right shows the Shroud as it would be seen by the naked eye. The image on the left is the negative from a grayscale photograph taken of the Shroud itself.

Contradicting the ^{14}C dating, work done by Dr. Alan Whanger demonstrated 170 points of congruence between the face on the Shroud and that on a 7TH century coin, and 145 points for a sixth century icon. Only 45 to 60 points of congruence are required to establish the identity or same source of face images in a court of law. (Stevenson and Habermas, 1990)

You, as the reader of this, may draw your own conclusions as to the reality of the image of the man on the Shroud of Turin. Suffice it to say that both authors were convinced that this was the image of Yeshua of Nazareth the first time they saw a positive of the face of the man on the Shroud. This was an epiphany for both of us, and was part of the impetus in writing this book, the other chief stimulus being, of course, our obtaining a copy of Bucke's thesis, *Cosmic Consciousness*. It is not an overstatement to say that Bucke's work convinced both of us as to the true nature of Christ, and therefore the key to understanding Yeshua and his mind: his possession of Christ Consciousness.

The remainder of this work will be devoted to an exegesis of these remarks. Let the reader be warned: some of this is heavy stuff.

Bibliography

Bucke, Richard Maurice. *Cosmic Consciousness: A Study in the Evolution of the Human Mind*. Copyright 1900 by Innes & Sons; copyright 1922 by Edward P. A. Connaughton; copyright 1923 by E. P. Dutton & Co.; New York: paperback by E. P. Dutton & Co., Inc., 1969; hardcover by Causeway Books, 1974.

Heller, John. *Report on the Shroud of Turin*. Boston: Houghton Mifflin, 1983.

Stevenson, Kenneth E., and Gary R. Habermas. *Verdict on the Shroud*. Ann Arbor, MI: Servant, 1981.

—. *The Shroud and the Controversy*. Nashville, TN: Thomas Nelson, 1990.

Williams, Peter S. "The Shroud of Turin: A Cumulative Case for Authenticity." Online resource located at the following URL: http://www.case.edu.au/images/uploads/03_pdfs/williams-shroud-turin.pdf

Wilson, Ian. *The Blood and the Shroud*. New York: Simon & Schuster, 1998.

~ ✿ ~

1921 Templar Church in Bethlehem of Galilee

Bethlehem of Galilee dates back thousands of years, having been one of the first Jewish towns mentioned in the bible and a Christian village during the Crusades. Modern Bethlehem of Galilee was built in 1906 by German Templars who revitalized it as a farming settlement. They remained until the outbreak of World War II, when the British placed local Germans into internment camps, eventually either repopulating them to Australia or sending them back to Germany. In 1948, Bethlehem of Galilee was converted into a *Moshav*, an Israeli cooperative agricultural community, which it remains to this day.

—Kontera Israel Blog at www.blog.kontera.com

Chapter 2

The Consciousness of Christ

HE CENTRAL THESIS of this book is that Yeshua possessed Christ consciousness, and that possession of this faculty alone is sufficient to explain who he was, what he did, and why he did it. There is nothing supernatural about this state of awareness; preternatural perhaps—in the sense that it is beyond the usual or normal, that it is extraordinary—but nothing more. A person blessed with Christ consciousness simply becomes aware of things about which most of us haven't even a clue. You need not believe in gods descending to earth or virgin births in order to grasp the significance of Yeshua of Nazareth when viewed in this context. Books and other texts have been written about this man in almost uncountable numbers, and the number of reasons for his greatness set forth by the writers of these texts is nearly as great. These range from the fantastic theory that he was the incarnation of the second person of a trinity, which is the ultimate development of Christian mythology, to ridiculous theories such as that he had eidetic vision, and that this explained everything about him.

As we shall see, the earliest tradition, or *Christology*, about Yeshua held that he was adopted by God as a "special son" at the time of his baptism by John. Our theory is that Yeshua became Christ conscious at this time, and that this accounts for why little or nothing is known about him prior to that time (the only canonical account of him before that time, the story about his discoursing with the priests in the temple at the age of 12, is widely believed by biblical scholars to be apocryphal—a myth [Luke 2:40–50]).

How can it be that the mere possession of a state of consciousness, albeit an extraordinary one, can account for someone as spectacular as Yeshua of Nazareth? In order to answer this question we must describe what Christ consciousness is—to the extent that it *can* be described. To do this, we must begin with basics.

What is consciousness?

To explain what we mean by "Christ consciousness" we must first define what we mean by "consciousness." We do not mean the simple dichotomy between consciousness and unconsciousness. We use the word—as Bucke did—to indicate a state of awareness. Most living creatures are aware of their environment. But even a casual appraisal reveals a tremendous difference between the awareness of an insect and that of a human being. In addition, most of us would agree that there is a categorical difference between the awareness of most animals and that of a human being. To explain such a difference we must postulate the existence of more than a single state of consciousness. We begin by describing two states of consciousness, which differ in the nature of the awareness that they confer upon the creatures possessing them. We call these states—as did Bucke—simple consciousness and self consciousness.

How do we define these states of consciousness?

Simple consciousness

This is the nature of the awareness of most animals. Even very primitive animals, such as insects, are aware of the environment around them. If a mosquito sitting on your arm sees your hand approaching, it will attempt to fly away to avoid being squashed. Scientists call such behavior "instinctual." Some creatures possessing simple consciousness are, however, capable of much more complex thinking. Many advanced species have thought processes that cannot be described simply as instinctual. For example, a man once observed a dog running with a long stick in his mouth rotate his head in order to pass through a narrow opening. The dog required a certain level of reasoning to realize that holding the stick horizontally would result in a disaster when the stick collided with the sides of the opening. Also, many animals are capable of learning how to do new things, and learned behavior is by definition not instinctual.

Simple consciousness comprises a range of levels from that of extremely primitive creatures through that of primates, including— as we shall see—even human beings on occasion. How do we define a state of consciousness that encompasses such a vast range of different levels of awareness? As it turns out, the easiest way is to define simple consciousness as "not self consciousness." This is because the salient difference between the two states of consciousness is a lack of self awareness in the state of simple consciousness. A state of simple consciousness does not include an awareness of self as an object. To describe this more precisely we must define what we mean by self consciousness and how it differs from simple consciousness.

Self consciousness

This is the nature of the awareness of most adult human beings. In ordinary conversation the term "self-conscious" refers to a heightened state of self awareness, usually caused by embarrassment. This is not what we mean. Rather, we are using the term in its primary dictionary meaning: Aware of oneself as an individual or of one's own being, actions, or thoughts.[†] Self consciousness allows one to realize that he is a being who lives in a world among other beings. Simple consciousness *knows;* self consciousness *knows that it knows.*

[†] *The American Heritage® Dictionary of the English Language, Third Edition* copyright © 1992 by Houghton Mifflin Company. Electronic version licensed from INSO Corporation. All rights reserved.

Simple consciousness can love, as anyone with a pet can testify, but only self consciousness is capable of thinking *I am loving my cat*. It is only the self conscious faculty that is able to say with Descartes, "*Cogito ergo sum*"—I think, therefore I am. This state of consciousness is restricted almost exclusively to humans. Animals—with the exception of a few of the brightest members of the high primates (chimpanzees, gorillas, and orangutans)—do not think this way. A cat walking on a garden path is certainly aware of its surroundings and of the act of walking but is apparently not capable of thinking to itself, "I am a cat walking along this garden path"—either verbally or non-verbally. Such thoughts are reserved for creatures that possess self consciousness: human beings.

The dog in our earlier example did not think to itself, *If I try to go through this fence with the stick held horizontally I am going to come to grief. I'd better hold it vertically so it will fit through the opening*. Rather, the dog probably anticipated a collision with the stick in a horizontal position and simply took action—possibly in part instinctual—to correct the problem.

Bucke defines self consciousness by contrasting it with simple consciousness, as in the following:

> By means of [simple consciousness] a dog or horse is just as conscious of the things around him as a man is; he is also conscious of his own limbs and body and he knows that these are a part of himself. Over and above this Simple Consciousness, which is possessed by man as by animals, man has another which is called Self Consciousness. By virtue of this faculty man is not only conscious of trees, rocks, waters, his own limbs and body, but he becomes conscious of himself as a distinct entity apart from all the rest of the universe. It is as good as certain that no animal can realize himself in that way. Further, by means of self consciousness, man (who knows as the animal knows) becomes capable of treating his own mental states as objects of consciousness. The animal is, as it were, immersed in his consciousness as a fish in the sea; he cannot, even in imagination, get outside of it for one moment so as to

realize it. But man by virtue of self consciousness can step aside, as it were, from himself and think: "Yes, that thought that I had about that matter is true; I know it is true and I know that I know it is true."

> —Bucke, R. M., *Cosmic Consciousness*, 1900, page 1.

Yet another authority implicitly draws much the same distinction between the two states:

> [An animal] has consciousness; i.e., it knows itself and its weal and woe; also the object which produces these; but its knowledge remains constantly subjective, never becomes objective: everything that it embraces appears to exist in and of itself, and can therefore never become an object of representation nor a problem for meditation. Its consciousness is thus wholly immanent.
>
> —Ward, Lester F., "Relation of Sociology to Anthropology,"
> *The American Anthropologist*, July 1895
> Quoted by Bucke, R. M., *Cosmic Consciousness*, 1900, p. 20.

Self consciousness is a radically different state of awareness. It changes everything. A self-conscious being experiences the external world in a wholly different way than a simple-conscious creature. Self consciousness is, as the saying goes, a whole new ball game.

One of the most mysterious features of self consciousness is its self-verifying nature. If blessed with unusually good fortune, people are supposed to pinch themselves to make sure they are not dreaming. But have you ever had to pinch yourself to be sure you were awake? We thought not. Once you are thoroughly awake you know you are not dreaming. You require no external stimulus to convince you of this.

Simple consciousness is, however, not self-verifying. We know this because all of us experience simple consciousness while dreaming. While dreaming we generally do not know we are dreaming. We are immersed in a world where we react to things without really thinking about it, and where we take action often without knowing why we are doing it. The most amazing things happen to us in dreams without

triggering any suspicion on our part. For example, we think nothing
of it when the car we are driving abruptly becomes a bicycle. If we
were self-conscious such an event would cause us either to question
our sanity or to believe that we were dreaming.[†] But in our dreaming
state of simple consciousness we simply accept bizarre occurrences as
part of the way things are. We don't know that we are dreaming. We
only realize we were dreaming after we awaken and self consciousness
returns. On those rare occasions when self consciousness asserts itself
during a dream, it comes as a sudden flash of insight wherein the
dreamer realizes he is dreaming and that what is happening to him is
not real. It's almost like waking up while you are still asleep dreaming.
Again, this is self-verifying. No one has to tell the dreamer this; it is
immediately obvious to him. We shall return to this point later.

The nearly universal possession of self consciousness by adult
human beings constitutes the most definitive difference between our
species and the rest of the animal kingdom. Strangely, this point is
seldom appreciated even by scientists. Most often such derivative
attributes as the ability to make and use tools or the use of language
to communicate are taken as the dividing line between mankind
and the rest of the animals. But these behavioral icons have been
falling like dominoes. Jane Goodall's work has shown that chimpanzees know how to make tools suitable for a particular purpose.
Koko, the gorilla who learned American Sign Language, shows a fair
proficiency in the use of language to communicate (although one
can certainly argue that she shows evidence of self consciousness,
since she regularly refers to herself). Despite the panic caused by the
fall of these differences, people in general and scientists in particular
fail to use the concept of self consciousness to define the human
condition. Even though pioneers like Bucke showed the way about a
century ago, self awareness has not caught on as the best way to

---

[†] One of the authors once had a dream in which just such a bizarre occurrence
triggered a suspicion that he might be dreaming, which in turn caused a sudden
rise into the self conscious state, terminating the dream. In a case like this it
seems that one must have been on the verge of self consciousness before such a
suspicion could have occurred in the first place.

describe the consciousness of human beings. Yet all of the things that make us human depend on this state of consciousness: our abilities to judge good and evil; to empathize (put ourselves in someone else's place), and to conceive of a power higher than ourselves (God); our sense of modesty; our nagging consciences. A simple-conscious creature would not and could not do, be, or have any of these things. Animals are neither ashamed of nor aware of their nakedness. Self consciousness is surely the prerequisite for a sense of modesty. Self consciousness is both the first cause and the hallmark of what we call the human condition.

This was recognized at least one hundred years ago:

> Self consciousness is often referred to as a distinguishing characteristic of man. Many, however, fail to gain a clear conception of what this faculty is. Dr. [Edward] Carpenter confounds it with the "power of reflecting on their own mental states," while Mr. [Charles] Darwin associates it with abstraction and other of the derivative faculties. It is certainly something much simpler than introspection, and has an earlier origin than the highly derivative speculative faculties. If it could only be seized and clearly understood, *self consciousness would doubtless prove to be the primary and fundamental human attribute.* [emphasis added]
>
> —*Ibid.*, pp. 19-20.

Perhaps the difficulty of precisely defining self consciousness—in Lester's words, "if it could only be seized and clearly understood"— is the reason it is not more universally used to define the consciousness of human beings. This difficulty does not, however, prevent us from using self awareness to describe the state of ordinary human waking consciousness.

HOWEVER MAGNIFICENT self consciousness may be when compared with simple consciousness, there is yet a higher level of consciousness that has arisen in numerous individuals throughout the course of human history. This faculty we call Christ consciousness.

Christ consciousness

If describing the self consciousness that all of us experience during virtually every minute of of our waking lives is difficult—as we have seen that it is—we come now to a task enormously more formidable. How can we describe a state of consciousness that is as elevated above self consciousness as that faculty is above simple consciousness? The answer is that we can't. We cannot directly describe Christ consciousness using a language developed by self aware beings for use by the self conscious. As superb a tool as our language is when used to describe the actions and thoughts of ordinary human beings, it is a dismal failure when used to attempt a description of this level of consciousness that is so far removed from our everyday experience. What we must do instead is describe the manifestations of Christ consciousness as they are observed by ordinary human beings and some not-so-ordinary human beings, namely those who themselves have experienced for at least a brief period of time some degree of Christ consciousness.

We begin with Richard Maurice Bucke himself. Here is Bucke's description of his own brief experience of Christ consciousness—which he called Cosmic Consciousness—as told in his own words. We have taken the liberty of substituting the first person for the archaic third person originally used by Bucke, a literary device which is no longer in use although it was accepted practice when he wrote this.

> It was in the early spring in the beginning of my thirty-sixth year. I and two friends had spent the evening reading Wordsworth, Shelley, Keats, Browning, and especially Whitman. We parted at midnight, and I had a long drive in a hansom (it was in an English city). My mind, deeply under the influence of the ideas, images, and emotions called up by the reading and talk of the evening, was calm and peaceful. I was in a state of quiet, almost passive enjoyment. All at once, without warning of any kind, I found myself wrapped around as it were by a flame-colored cloud. For an instant I thought of fire, some sudden

conflagration in the great city, the next I knew that the light was within myself. Directly afterwards came upon me a sense of exultation, of immense joyousness accompanied or immediately followed by an intellectual illumination quite impossible to describe. Into my brain streamed one momentary lightning-flash of the Brahmic Splendor which has ever since lighted my life; upon my heart fell one drop of Brahmic Bliss, leaving thenceforward for always an aftertaste of heaven. Among other things I did not come to believe, I saw and knew that the Cosmos is not dead matter but a living Presence, that the soul of man is immortal, that the universe is so built and ordered that without any [doubt] all things work together for the good of each and all, that the foundation principle of the world is what we call love, and that the happiness of everyone is in the long run absolutely certain. I learned more within the few seconds during which the illumination lasted than in previous months or even years of study, and I learned much that no study could ever have taught.

The illumination itself continued not more than a few moments, but its effects proved ineffaceable; it was impossible for me to ever forget what I at that time saw and knew, neither did I, nor could I, ever doubt the truth of what was then presented to my mind.

—Bucke, Richard Maurice, *op. cit.*, pp. 7-8;
doubt substituted for the archaic *peradventure.*

FOLLOWING INTENSIVE STUDY of others throughout history who had apparently had an experience similar to his, Bucke developed a set of characteristics that served to define those who attain what he called Cosmic Consciousness. Here we have rearranged the manifestations listed by Bucke into a somewhat more logical order: characteristics of the onset of Christ consciousness, changes in the person's nature and perceptions, some secondary characteristics, and two others that we found to be doubtful.

Characteristics of the onset of Christ consciousness:
- ❑ Occurrence of the subjective light.
- ❑ Suddenness of the awakening.

Changes in the nature of a person attaining Christ consciousness:
- ❑ A dramatic intellectual illumination.
- ❑ A marked elevation of the moral sense.
- ❑ Transfiguration of the person as seen by others when Christ consciousness is actually present.
- ❑ Increased charisma.

Changes in the perceptions of one attaining Christ consciousness:
- ❑ A sense of immortality.
- ❑ Loss of all fear of death.
- ❑ Loss of any sense of sin.

Secondary characteristics, used by Bucke in his analysis of cases:
- ❑ After illumination, the person goes into seclusion, apparently to sort things out.
- ❑ The person is tempted to use Christ consciousness for personal gain, but rejects this.
- ❑ The person now sees the universe as divine and learns ineffable things.

Characteristics listed by Bucke that are, in our judgment, doubtful:
- ❑ Previous character of the person—intellectual, moral, and physical (the last is especially suspect).
- ❑ The person's age at illumination.

In *Cosmic Consciousness*, Bucke examines 14 cases of full-blown Christ consciousness comprising these individuals, who are listed here in chronological order by date of birth.

1. Gautama the Buddha
2. Jesus [Yeshua] the Christ
3. Paul the Apostle
4. Plotinus
5. Mohammed
6. Dante Alighieri
7. Bartolomé Las Casas
8. John Yepes
9. Francis Bacon
10. Jacob Behmen
11. William Blake
12. Honoré de Balzac
13. Walt Whitman
14. Edward Carpenter

Bucke examined 35 more cases, which he called "additional—some of them lesser, imperfect, and doubtful instances," of which he considered 29 to be genuine. These included, again in birth order, Moses, Gideon, Isaiah, Li R (Lao Tzu), Socrates, Roger Bacon (William Shakespeare), Blaise Pascal, Benedict Spinoza, James Gardiner, Emanuel Swedenborg, William Wordsworth, Charles G. Finney, Alexander Pushkin, Ralph Waldo Emerson, Alfred Lord Tennyson, Henry Thoreau, Ramakrisana Paramahansa, Richard Jefferies, J. William Lloyd, Horace Traubel, Paul Tyner, and 14 other individuals listed only by initials who wished to remain anonymous.

For each one of these proposed cases of Cosmic Consciousness, Bucke examined the available evidence, looking for correspondence between the accounts of each case and the items in the preceding list of manifestations. We discuss this list in connection with Bucke's analysis of his cases.

Occurrence of the subjective light

The subjective light is seen only at the time of illumination and, as the name implies, is normally only seen by the subject. In a very few instances—notably with Saint John of the Cross (John Yepes) and Yeshua—the subjective light may be seen by others and thus become objective (see Transfiguration, below). Bucke found evidence for the subjective light in six of his fourteen primary cases; it was implied in four other cases.

Suddenness of the awakening

Christ consciousness comes suddenly. Its manifestation has been described by some of its recipients as like a flash of lightning on a dark night, which instantly illuminates a hitherto unseen landscape. Bucke found direct evidence of this suddenness in eleven of his fourteen primary cases.

Intellectual illumination

The recipient of Christ consciousness experiences a dramatic intellectual illumination. In cases where little or nothing is known of the subject before the awakening—and this happens quite often, as one might suppose—any judgment of this must be necessarily subjective. In other cases, however, the effect is quite dramatic. Walt Whitman, for example, went from writing literally trivial pieces in the 1840s to writing the first edition of *Leaves of Grass* in the 1850s, which Bucke describes as having "pages across which in letters of ethereal fire are written the words ETERNAL LIFE." (*Ibid.*, page 187.) Bucke found evidence of this intellectual illumination in all fourteen of his primary cases.

Moral elevation

The recipient of Christ consciousness also undergoes a marked elevation in moral standards. Again, where the subject is unknown prior to illumination this must be judged subjectively. The loftiness of the subject's moral standards when compared with those of ordinary humans is, however, usually striking. For example, consider the "turn the other cheek" moral standard advocated by Yeshua. How many people do you know who agree with this, let alone practice it? Bucke found moral elevation evident in all fourteen of his primary cases.

Transfiguration

At times when Christ consciousness is actually present the subject may appear to glow (radiate light). This light may even appear to radiate from the clothes the subject is wearing. The haloes employed by artists when depicting holy persons are believed to be derived from this effect. Bucke found evidence of transfiguration in five of his primary cases (one case was doubtful); evidence of the occurrence of transfiguration in the case of the Apostle Paul is presented later in this chapter. Such evidence in the case of Walt Whitman came from an eyewitness, a Miss Helen Price, who was personally known to Dr. Bucke:

> One evening in 1866, while Walt Whitman was stopping with us in New York, the tea bell had been rung ten minutes or more when he came down from his room, and we all gathered around the table. I remarked him as he entered the room; there

seemed to be a *peculiar brightness* and elation about him, an almost irrepressible joyousness, which *shone from his face* and seemed to pervade his whole body. It was the more noticeable as his ordinary mood was one of quiet, yet cheerful serenity. I knew he had been working at a new edition of his book, and I hoped if he had an opportunity he would say something to let us into the secret of his mysterious joy. Unfortunately most of those at the table were occupied with some subject of conversation; at every pause I waited eagerly for him to speak; but no, someone else would begin again, until I grew almost wild with impatience and vexation. He appeared to listen, and would even laugh at some of the remarks that were made, yet he did not utter a single word during the meal; and his face still wore that *singular brightness* and delight, as though he had partaken of some divine elixir. His expression was so remarkable that I might have doubted my own observation had it not been noticed by another as well as myself.

—Bucke, R. M., *Cosmic Consciousness*, 1900; p. 195,
emphasis added.

Increased charisma

This characteristic seems weaker than the rest, and in almost all cases evidence of it must be subjective. Yet this subjective evidence can be very convincing. Testimony as to the charismatic nature of those who comprise most of Bucke's cases of "Cosmic Consciousness" is nearly overwhelming, although Bucke makes a point of it in only six or seven of his fourteen primary cases. Yeshua was certainly charismatic, to say the least about him.

Sense of immortality

Awakened subjects know they are immortal, apparently in same way that an ordinary person knows when he is awake and not dreaming. Bucke found this sense of immortality in fully twelve of his fourteen primary cases.

Loss of the fear of death

This would seem to be a necessary concomitant of the sense of immortality conferred by Christ consciousness, but it goes further than that. Not only is there no fear of death but there is no fear of dying in those who are blessed with this state of consciousness. In the words of the Apostle Paul, "Death, where is your sting?" [1 Cor 15:55]. Bucke found this attribute in twelve of his fourteen primary cases (doubtful in one).

Loss of any sense of sin

Upon illumination the subject's sense of sin is obliterated. It is not that the subject finds that his sins are forgiven but that there were never any sins to have been forgiven. In Bucke's words, the subject "no longer sees that there is any sin in the world from which to escape." (Bucke, Richard M., *op. cit.*, page 62.) Bucke found this characteristic well marked in seven of his fourteen primary cases, and probably present in three others.

Retreat into seclusion

Apparently the onset of Christ consciousness is such a shock to its recipients that many of them are driven into seclusion for a period of time in order to understand what has happened to them. Details about such a flight are lacking in most of the cases Bucke examined. The best-known example is that of Yeshua, who retreated into the desert for "forty days" following his illumination. Evidence for such a retreat is also found in the cases of the Apostle Paul and Gautama the Buddha.

Resists temptation

The newly illuminated may be tempted to use the knowledge conferred on them by Christ consciousness for personal gain, but the elevated moral sense that accompanies this knowledge causes them to reject the temptation. This is most remarkable in the cases of Buddha—who was tempted by Mara, "the evil one"—and Christ, who was tempted by Satan. Bucke found weak evidence for such resisted temptation in two more of his fourteen primary cases.

Sees the universe as divine and learns ineffable things

Christ consciousness reveals a divine world—"a living Presence," in Bucke's words. Yeshua called this world "the kingdom of God." Whitman wrote, "I hear and behold God in every object" ("Song of Myself," in *Leaves of Grass*, 1855). Some of what is revealed is ineffable—incapable of being expressed in words. Writing of an episode of Christ consciousness, the Apostle Paul says that he "heard unspeakable things, things that a man may not utter" [2 Cor 12:4]. Whitman writes, "I am charged with untold and untellable wisdom" ("Of the Terrible Doubt of Appearances," *Leaves of Grass*, 1860). Bucke found evidence of these effects in nine of his fourteen primary cases.

Doubtful characteristics

The prior intellectual and moral character of those receiving Christ consciousness may or may not be significant; we are not convinced that they are. The subject's physical condition is most likely irrelevant. Christ consciousness is a mental state not a physical condition. After all, Stephen Hawking is one of the most brilliant theoretical physicists in the world today, yet his physical condition is abysmal. As to the age of the recipient, most of those Bucke studied were in their thirties at the time of illumination. But life expectancy was fifty years or less during the period covered (500 BC through the 19th century), so one would hardly expect a much different result.

Additional confirmation

A century has elapsed since Bucke wrote *Cosmic Consciousness*. During that time some additional source material has surfaced that supports Bucke's analysis. These include evidence of the reality of two of Bucke's primary cases, William Blake and the Apostle Paul, a possible new case, Leslie Weatherhead, who lived in the twentieth century, and an old case, Meister Eckhart, a medieval mystic.

William Blake

Bucke states that nothing is known about the illumination of William Blake, one of his primary cases of cosmic consciousness.

Here is the missing information, contained in an untitled poem
Blake included in a letter to a friend of his, one Thomas Butts, dated
October 2, 1800. We reproduce this poem in its entirety; comments
are in italics to the right of Blake's text.

To my Friend Butts I write
My first Vision of Light,   *Blake's first experience of Christ consciousness*
On the yellow sands sitting.
The Sun was Emitting
His glorious beams
From Heaven's high Streams.
Over Sea, over Land
My eyes did Expand   *His consciousness begins to expand*
Into regions of air
Away from all Care,   *Earthly cares fall away*
Into regions of fire
Remote from Desire;   *Interest in material things disappears*
The Light of the Morning
Heaven's Mountains adorning;
In particles bright
The jewels of Light   *The subjective light appears*
Distinct shone & clear.
Amaz'd & in fear   *As usual, he is not sure what is happening to him*
I each particle gazed,
Astonish'd, Amazed;
For each was a Man
Human-form'd. Swift I ran,
For they beckon'd to me
Remote by the Sea,
Saying: "Each grain of Sand,
Every Stone on the Land
Each rock & each hill,
Each fountain & rill,
Each herb & each tree,
Mountain, hill, earth & sea,
Cloud, Meteor & Star,

Are Men seen Afar."   *The world and people form a single, living reality*
I stood in the Streams
Of Heaven's bright beams,   *He stands in the subjective light*
And saw Felpham sweet   *Felpham is the town where this happened*
Beneath my bright feet   *The subjective light shines on his feet*
In soft Female charms;
And in her fair arms
My Shadow I knew
And my wife's shadow too,
And my Sister & Friend.   *He sees all humanity in this vision*
We like infants descend
In our Shadows on Earth,
Like a weak mortal birth.   *Ordinary existence is a pale shadow of reality*
My eyes more and more
Like a Sea without shore
Continue Expanding,   *His consciousness keeps expanding*
The Heavens commanding,
Till the Jewels of Light,
Heavenly Men beaming bright,
Appear'd as One Man,   *He now sees all of humanity as a single divine being*
Who complacent began
My limbs to infold   *The Christ sense takes 'possession' of him*
In his beams of bright gold;   *The subjective light continues*
Like dross purg'd away
All my mire and my clay.   *He loses his senses of sin and mortality*
Soft consum'd in delight
In his bosom Sun bright   *The subjective light, again*
I remain'd. Soft he smil'd,
And I heard his voice Mild
Saying: "This is My Fold,
O thou Ram horn'd with gold,
Who awakest from Sleep   *Compares this to awakening*
On the Sides of the Deep.   *He wakens to Christ consciousness at the shore*
On the Mountains around
The roarings resound

Of the lion & wolf,
The loud Sea & deep gulf,
These are guards of My fold,
O thou Ram horn'd with gold!"
And the voice faded mild.
I remain'd as a Child;   *In other words, he has been reborn*
All I ever had known
Before me bright Shone.   *He sees his life in the light of Christ consciousness*
I saw you & your wife
By the fountains of Life.   *The ultimate good of all beings is assured*
Such the Vision to me
Appear'd by the sea.

Virtually all of the characteristics of the coming of Christ conscious-ness are present in this poem. The subjective light is well marked, with numerous references throughout the text, as is the expansion of consciousness. Loss of both his sense of sin (*mire*) and his fear of death (*clay*) are explicitly stated. He implies the feeling of rebirth: the new being is like a child. Everything he has known in his former life is now revealed in the new light of Christ consciousness to be— as Yeshua put it—part of the kingdom of God. He apparently hears some noise with his experience ("roarings resound"), something that is new in this description. In any event, Blake's place in this august company seems assured.

The Apostle Paul

Bucke gives no evidence of transfiguration in the case of Paul, probably because he had no access to such information. In the apocryphal *Acts of Paul and Thecla*, however, we find the following description of Paul.

> At length they saw a man coming (namely Paul), of a low stature, bald (or shaved) on the head, crooked thighs, hand-some legs, hollow-eyed; had a crooked nose; full of grace; for sometimes he appeared as a man, sometimes he had the countenance of an angel.
>
> —*Acts of Paul and Thecla* 1:7

This description has the appearance of one of those tidbits of fact that many authors of apocryphal works inserted in their writings to improve their chances of being believed. The words "sometimes he had the countenance of an angel" seem to be a direct reference to periods of transfiguration.

Leslie Weatherhead

Dr. Weatherhead was a Christian writer of considerable aptitude. Anyone who has read his works is familiar with his keen mind and superb spiritual outlook. He apparently had several experiences of Christ consciousness not unlike the one Bucke describes of himself. He wrote:

> I could not call myself a mystic, but on half a dozen occasions I have had experiences which *for me* made me certain of the reality of some supernatural Entity which, or whom, I label "God."
>
> —Weatherhead, Leslie. D., *The Christian Agnostic*, p. 74.

Here is his account of one of those experiences; it occurred when he was nineteen years old and took place on a train passing through the Vauxhall Bridge Station in London.

> For a few seconds only, I suppose, the whole compartment filled with light. This is the only way I know in which to describe the moment, for there was nothing to *see* at all. I felt caught up into some tremendous sense of being with a loving, triumphant and shining purpose. I never felt more humble. I never felt more exalted. A most curious, but overwhelming sense possessed me and filled me with ecstasy. I felt that all was well for all mankind—how poor the words seem! The word "well" is so poverty stricken. All men were shining and glorious beings who in the end would enter incredible joy. Beauty, music, joy, love immeasurable and a glory unspeakable, all this they would inherit. Of this they were heirs. My puny message, if I passed my exams and qualified as a minister, would contribute only an infinitesimal drop to the ocean of love and truth which God wanted men to enjoy, but my message was of the same

nature as that ocean. . . . in that hour I knew the ministry was the right path for me. . . . An indescribable joy possessed me. . . .

All this happened over fifty years ago but even now I can see myself in the corner of that dingy, third-class compartment with the feeble lights of inverted gas mantles overhead and the Vauxhall platforms outside with milk cans standing there. In a few moments the glory had departed—all but one curious, lingering feeling. I *loved* everybody in that compartment. . . . They seemed—all of them—immensely lovable and valuable. I seemed to sense the golden worth in them all. I knew then— and believe now—that God would not allow any one of his children finally to miss the ecstatic happiness and joy towards which every human life, in spite of a million deviations, hindrances, wrong choices and the following of false signposts, is moving. . . . No one who has had such an experience can ever doubt but that in the end good will triumph over every form of evil, and that every life, however humble, frustrated indifferent or even careless, is in the care of this Power and within a Plan, vast beyond our power to imagine, which will work out in a blessedness which brings utter satisfaction and a quality of bliss for which there are no words.

—*Ibid.*, pp. 75-77.

The reader should compare this account by Leslie Weatherhead with the description by Richard Bucke of his own experience of a "flash" of Christ consciousness, which appears on his page five. In particular, the final sentence of Weatherhead's account is so much like Bucke's words, "I saw and knew that the Cosmos is not dead matter but a living Presence, that the soul of man is immortal, that the universe is so built and ordered that without any doubt all things work together for the good of each and all, . . . and that the happiness of everyone is in the long run absolutely certain," that in today's world it might even be taken as evidence of plagiarism. Just this one example of parallelism surely should be enough to convince the reader that there is certainly some common thread that runs through experiences of this kind.

Meister Eckhart

The sermons and writings of Johannes "Master" Eckhart (1260–ca 1328), a German Dominican priest, are sufficient to establish him as a probable case of Christ consciousness. Nearly all of the characteristics listed for this state of consciousness are depicted in his writings in one place or another. The reader should examine Eckhart's sermons and other printed works, which will confirm the truth of this statement (see references).

Summary of Christ consciousness

Bucke's thesis—and ours—is that a third state of consciousness exists, one as far removed from ordinary waking self consciousness as that is from the simple consciousness of beasts. Although this state of consciousness has occurred in only a mere handful of individuals throughout the course of history, its characteristics are well marked. They consist of the following, which is a summary of our discussion up to this point.

Christ consciousness comes to the subject suddenly—in a flash as it were—and is usually (always?) accompanied by a subjective light or glow that seems to emanate from the subject and normally can be seen only by the subject himself. This new state of consciousness reveals the world to be divine, not a dead but a living thing, in which the ultimate good of every living creature is assured.[†] In this respect the onset of Christ consciousness can be likened to the coming of self consciousness in a dream—to which we alluded earlier—wherein the dream world is revealed instantly to be a sham, not at all what it appeared to be merely a moment before. This likeness has been remarked by others; Kahlil Gibran wrote about Zoroaster, saying that he "woke from man's ancient sleep and stood at the bed of our dreaming." [*Jesus the Son of Man*, 1928]

After this sudden illumination, the subject is left in an entirely altered state. Besides the knowledge that has been imparted, the

---

[†] Paul writes that "all things work good for those who love God" [Rom 8:28]; not that things work good only for those who love God, but that only those who love God—those who have the indwelling Christ—can see this is true.

subject now displays a moral sense that is far superior to that of ordinary humans. He is aware of his own immortality as well as that of others, which they themselves do not recognize; he therefore loses all fear of death or dying. The subject also loses any sense of sin—not that his sins have been forgiven, but that there are none to be forgiven.

Immediately after his illumination the subject is liable to go into seclusion, apparently to think things out and attempt to understand what has happened to him. If tempted to use Christ consciousness for personal gain, he rejects this as incompatible with what he has learned from his new faculty. After returning to the company of others, an increased charisma is apparent. The subject normally (always?) believes that he can help others to attain the same consciousness that he now enjoys, and often takes to preaching or writing with this end in mind. Christ consciousness is not usually continuous, but comes and goes, as if the subject were capable of this second-level awakening for only brief periods of time, after which he returns to the normal self-conscious state. During periods of actual Christ consciousness he may appear transfigured, appearing to glow when observed by others. The subject usually refers to the Christ sense as if it were a separate person (e.g., Whitman's "the other that I am," Dante's "Beatrice," Yeshua's "Son of man").

Bucke writes of those who have possessed Christ consciousness:

> The better known members of this group who, were they collected together, could be accommodated all at one time in a modern [living] room, have created all the great modern religions, beginning with Taoism and Buddhism, and speaking generally have created, through religion and literature, modern civilization. . . . [They] dominate the last twenty-five, especially the last five, centuries as stars of the first magnitude dominate the midnight sky.
>
> —Bucke, R. M., *Cosmic Consciousness*, 1900; p 9.

In the chapters that follow we shall develop evidence that Yeshua had Christ consciousness, as defined here, and show that this form of consciousness is both necessary and sufficient to explain the things that he is reported to have done and said.

References

Acts of Paul and Thecla, The. In the apocrypha; cf. *The Lost Books of the Bible and the Forgotten Books of Eden,* a Fountain Book. Cleveland: William Collins & World Publishing Co., 34TH printing, 1977 (and many other editions).

Bible, New Testament: First and Second Corinthians, Romans; free translation from the Greek.

Blakney, Raymond B., translator. *Meister Eckhart: A Modern Translation.* New York: Harper & Row, 1941. There are numerous other compilations of the works of Eckhart, which the reader may find in almost any public library or on the internet in public domain works.

Bucke, Richard Maurice. *Cosmic Consciousness: A Study in the Evolution of the Human Mind.* Copyright 1900 by Innes & Sons; copyright 1922 by Edward P. A. Connaughton; copyright 1923 by E. P. Dutton & Co.; New York: paperback by E. P. Dutton & Co., Inc., 1969; hardcover by Causeway Books, 1974. (All of the page references herein refer to the Causeway Edition.)

Fleming, Ursula. *Meister Eckhart: The Man from whom God Hid Nothing.* Leominster, Herefordshire: Gracewing, 1995.

Gibran, Kahlil. *Jesus the Son of Man.* New York: Random House, 1928; Alfred A. Knopf, Inc., 29TH printing, March 1972.

McGinn, Bernard, and Edmund Colledge, editors & translators. *Meister Eckhart, The Essential Sermons, Commentaries, Treatises and Defense.* New York: Paulist Press, 1981.

Ward, Lester F. "Relation of Sociology to Anthropology." *The American Anthropologist,* July 1895. Quoted by Bucke. The article is available online at JStor: www.jstor.org/stable/658507

Weatherhead, Leslie D. *The Christian Agnostic.* Nashville: Abingdon Press, 1965; Festival Edition published October 1979.

Whitman, Walt. *Leaves of Grass.* Various editions beginning in 1855 and running through 1892; the actual date of each poem is given in the text reference.

Photo from the Internet

The village of Magdala on the Sea of Galilee

This was the home of Miriam of Magdala (Mary Magdalene) at the time of Yeshua's ministry in Israel.

Chapter 3
A Man Named Yeshua

ERE WE EXPLORE WHAT WE KNOW about the person around whom one of the world's great religions has grown. What, exactly, do we know about this person and where did he come from? Why do we know almost nothing about him except for a short period of time leading up to his crucifixion by the Romans?

What Do We Really Know about Yeshua?

The expert opinion of biblical scholars on how much we can say we really know about Yeshua has ranged between two extremes. On the one hand, there is the optimistic assumption that everything in the Gospels is literally true. On the other, there is the pessimistic verdict of the most radical members of the form-critical school that we know virtually nothing of the historical Yeshua. The consensus today lies somewhere near the midpoint of these extremes. We are concerned here, however, only with the rock-solid underpinnings of our knowledge about Yeshua. What are those facts about the historical Yeshua that we can say we know beyond a shadow of a doubt? Here is a list of the few things we can be certain of.

- ❑ Yeshua was a real person. His name was Yeshua bar[†] Yosef. He was born circa 2 BC and crucified by Pontius Pilatus (Pilate) circa 30 AD.

- ❑ Circa 29 AD he appeared in history as Yeshua of Nazareth, an itinerant preacher from Galilee. He preached in and around Galilee, attracted a following that included some (traditionally, twelve) disciples, and eventually traveled to Jerusalem where he was crucified.

- ❑ After he was gone his followers came to believe that in him they had seen God Himself.

- ❑ His followers were convinced that they saw Yeshua alive several days after he had been crucified and buried.

This may seem like a meager amount of knowledge to lay claim to, yet it forms a solid nucleus on which to build a picture of the historical Yeshua. The first point, that he was a real person, is no longer seriously in doubt. He was born around the time of the death of Herod the Great in 4 BC. Yeshua may have been born as early as 4 BC, although 2 BC is now the commonly accepted date and 1 BC may be more likely. The date of his crucifixion is more uncertain. If Yeshua was born in 2 BC he would have become thirty years old in 29 AD. A Jew was not considered mature enough to preach to others until he was 30 years old. Luke specifically says that Yeshua was "about thirty years old" when he was baptized by John [Lk 3:23]. Luke also states that John the Baptist began to preach "in the fifteenth year of Tiberius," which was 28-29 AD [Lk 3:1]. In the same year Herod Antipas, who later had John beheaded, came to power. The beginning of Yeshua's public ministry is therefore fixed around the same time. Since Tiberius became emperor of Rome on 19 September, 14 AD, most of his fifteenth year occurred in 29 AD. This is the most likely date for Yeshua's baptism by John. The date of his

---

[†] The word *bar* is Aramaic for "son of"; the equivalent in Hebrew is *ben*.

crucifixion depends on the length of his ministry, which is uncertain. The author of John and some early church fathers believed it was three years. The synoptic gospels and other Church Fathers believed that it was only one year (Irenaeus wrote that it was "only one year and a few months"—*De Principiis*, 4:5). The date of his death could therefore have been 30, 31, or 32 AD, depending on the elapsed time between the baptism and the crucifixion. If our chronology is correct—and it must be at least close—Yeshua was about 30 years old when he began his ministry and between 31 and 34 when he was crucified.

That Yeshua preached in and around Galilee, attracted crowds and some disciples, and went to Jerusalem where he was crucified is the kernel of the gospel stories. This much, at least, must be true. The third and fourth points are by far the most crucial of the lot. They comprise indirect evidence, to be sure, but they are also the core of the Christian religion. It is difficult for anyone to believe that these two statements are not true. Joseph Klausner, himself a Jew, writes in *Jesus of Nazareth*: "...it is impossible to suppose that there was any conscious deception: the nineteen hundred years' faith of millions is not founded on deception." No matter what we may believe is the truth about Yeshua, we must grant the accuracy of these two points. The Disciples, Apostles, and founding Fathers of the Christian Church must have believed they were true or there never would have been a Christian religion.

The Name of Yeshua

We in the West have been long accustomed to hearing the name Jesus Christ. Yet Jesus was not really his given name, and Christ is a title, not a name at all. The Aramaic name we have transformed into Jesus is actually pronounced "Yeshu" or "Yeshua" (Yeh-**shoo**-uh). Christ derives from Christos, which is a Greek translation of the Jewish title Meshiah (pronounced "Meh-**shy**-uh"). If we are to be accurate, whenever we see the word "Christ" in the gospel stories we should read "Messiah." For instance, Peter could not possibly have told Yeshua (in Mt 16:16) "You are the Christ, the Son of the living

God," because "Christ" is Greek and Peter was speaking Aramaic, and the idea that Christ was the Son of God had not even been conceived of then. What he undoubtedly did say was "You are the Meshiah"[†] (cf. Mk. 8:29). We must be constantly 'thinking Hebrew' as we read ancient sources.

The name of Yeshua's father, Joseph, is pronounced "Yosef." Yeshua's formal name was thus Yeshua bar Yosef in his native tongue, Aramaic, meaning "Yeshua the son of Yosef." We shall use the name Yeshua consistently in the rest of this book to avoid the connotations inherent in the name "Jesus."

How did Yeshua's name come to be so distorted in English? The source of this mistake goes back to the time when the only Bibles were written in Latin. After Martin Luther came on the scene, translations of the Bible were made for the first time in languages that most people could read. Since Luther was German, the first of these translations naturally was in his native tongue. In German the name used for Yeshua in the Latin Vulgate (*Iousu*) was spelled *Jesu*. When the king's scribes made the King James Bible many years later, they simply followed the German spelling, adding an 's' at the end. But in German, as in most Indo-European languages with the exception of English, the letter J is usually pronounced like an English Y or H. The German *Jesu* is pronounced much like English "Yeshu." But because the King James Bible spelled the name as Jesus, that became the accepted form in English. In this way we lost the original name of the person on whom Christianity is based.

For more on this, see "The name of Jesus: The mistransliteration of a Greek mistransliteration" in the Introduction (page x).

Where was Yeshua born?

The three Synoptic Gospels place Yeshua's birthplace in Bethlehem. John ducks the issue, but implies a Galilean birthplace:

> Hearing his words, some of the people said, "Surely this man is a prophet." Others said, "He is the Messiah." And yet others said, "How can the Messiah come from Galilee? Does scripture not say

---

† If Peter was speaking Aramaic, the word would have been *Mashiha*.

the Messiah will come from the family of David, and from Bethlehem, the village where David lived?" Therefore the people were divided because of Yeshua. [Jn 7:40-43].

John never rebuts this argument by writing, for example, "But he did come from Bethlehem—he was born there." Rather, he reinforces it:

> [Nicodemus] asked [the Pharisees], "Does our law condemn a man without hearing him first?" They replied, "Are you also from Galilee? Study this matter, and you will see that no prophet is to come out of Galilee." [Jn 7:51-52]

Today, most biblical scholars agree with John that Yeshua was born in Galilee. The nativity stories in the synoptic gospels are full of discrepancies and contradictions. For example, the census under Quirinius mentioned in Luke [2:2] took place long after Yeshua was born, and no census that required people to register in their home towns has ever been discovered. These nativity stories, while they make charming Christmas carols, are just that—myths. Why were they invented? For two reasons: to show that Yeshua was born in Bethlehem, where the Messiah was supposed to come from as a descendant of David, and to show that Yeshua was born divine. These things were required to support the divine birth Christology, which was not developed until many years after the Crucifixion. Because so much time had gone by, the Evangelists were forced to use guesswork in laying the foundations of their nativity stories. Much of the time they evidently guessed badly. In addition, recent research has shown that there was a Bethlehem (Beit L'hem) in Galilee, located only seven miles from Nazareth. This was undoubtedly the Bethlehem in which Yeshua was born (cf. Bruce Chilton, *Rabbi Jesus*, pp. 7–9).

None of this, however, matters much here. As you shall see, our interest in Yeshua starts at the time of his baptism by John. What he was like and what happened to him before then are of no importance. We believe—as do many others—that the reason so little is known of Yeshua prior to his baptism by John is that previously he was a rather ordinary person.

Was Yeshua really born of a virgin?

Current Christology holds that Yeshua was born of a virgin, who in turn was born of an "immaculate conception." This appears to non-believers as errant nonsense. The immaculate conception part is no doubt myth made up centuries later by the Catholic Church; nobody else really believes it. But the part about his mother Miriam (Mary) having been a virgin is not so easily dismissed. Bruce Chilton believes that Yeshua was the object of some derision for being a "*mamzer*"[1] (English: bastard) and referred to sardonically as "Yeshua bar Amma"—Yeshua the son of the Mother. Yet it is certainly not impossible that Miriam was technically a virgin after having conceived Yeshua.

Modern forensic techniques have revealed that it is possible for sperm to bypass the hymen (maidenhead) and fertilize a woman's egg. The hymen does not totally block the vagina. Premarital lovers in those ancient days when no kind of birth control was possible would sometimes engage in partial penetration and ejaculation by the man, without any conception occurring—most of the time. This could have been one of the times such a method failed. When Yosef discovered upon marrying Miriam that, even though she was obviously pregnant, she was still a virgin, it would have been natural for him to have supposed that something miraculous had occurred. Whether Yosef was Yeshua's father or not is immaterial here. Yeshua's parents would both have supposed that her conception had been somehow divinely accomplished.

Something of this nature could easily have given rise to the later tradition that Yeshua was born of a virgin.

The Baptism of Yeshua

The four evangelists, Mark, Matthew, Luke, and John, are seldom unanimous about anything in the gospel story. But one thing they all agree on: the Spirit of God "descended on Yeshua like a dove" at the time of his Baptism by John. Mark gives what is probably the earliest version of the episode.

> In those days Yeshua came from Nazareth of Galilee and
> was baptized by John in the Jordan. And when he came up out
> of the water, immediately he saw the heavens opened and the
> Spirit descending upon him like a dove; and a voice came
> from heaven, "You are my beloved Son; with you I am well
> pleased." [Mk 1:9-11]

John carefully avoids mention of the baptism itself but has John the
Baptist say that he saw the Spirit descend on Yeshua "as a dove from
heaven, and it remained on him" [Jn 1:32].

We are primarily concerned here with the words spoken to
Yeshua by the heavenly voice [Mk 1:11]. These comprise two quotations from the Old Testament: the part before the semicolon is from
Psalm 2:7, the second part, from Isaiah 42:1. Where did these words
come from? What is their significance?

Scholars generally agree that the information on his baptism could
have come only from Yeshua himself. Indeed, the lines immediately
following Mark 1:11 reflect information that could have come from no
one but Yeshua:

> The Spirit immediately drove him out into the wilderness.
> And he was in the wilderness forty days, tempted by Satan; and
> he was with the wild beasts; and the angels ministered to him.
> [Mk 1:12-13]

Since Yeshua was alone in the wilderness, no one else could have
related these things, whether or not they are accurately reported in
the gospels.

It is easy to imagine that most of the description in Mark 1:9-13
was supplied by Yeshua himself, but the heavenly voice in Mark 1:11 is
an exception to this. As it stands in Mark it would appear to be a simple Christological statement, perhaps taken from the kerygma of the
early church. If so, why does it appear here? Matthew and Luke both
report the words in exactly the same form. In the *Codex Bezae* and
some allied texts of Luke, however, the words are quoted as "You are
my beloved Son, today I have begotten you" [Lk 3:22; var]. This
appears to make more sense in the context. It is the full sentence

spoken by Yahweh in Psalm 2:7; the fragment from Isaiah drops out. Surprisingly, though, the variant readings in Luke appear to be a later redaction rather than a more original version of the text. Why would a scribe make a redaction in the third chapter of Luke that is in direct contradiction to the doctrine of the virgin birth of Yeshua presented in the first chapter? Indeed, unless the scribe knew of a genuine tradition antedating the text his action would have amounted to heresy.

We believe that this nameless scribe did indeed know of such a tradition, probably the same one used by the unknown author of the letter to the Hebrews. There we find strong evidence that the original tradition was different from that which is found in the gospels. This letter, possibly written before the gospels, supports the variant reading of Luke 3:22 in two places:

> For to what angel did God ever say, "You are my Son, today I have begotten you"? [Heb 1:5]

> [Yeshua] was appointed by Him who said to him, "You are my Son, today I have begotten you." [Heb 5:5]

Both Matthew and Luke were, however, obliged to change these words into the version now found in their gospels because they directly contradict the doctrine of Yeshua's virgin birth, which both authors include. Mark apparently knows nothing about the virgin birth, but whether or not his gospel ever contained the original tradition of the baptism is impossible to determine from the extant manuscripts. So much has been lost.

The tradition of the virgin birth of Yeshua represents an element of what we may call the 'divine origin Christology.' Within Catholicism, this theology ultimately led to such doctrines as the Immaculate Conception and the 'sinlessness' of Mary, the mother of Yeshua. The original version of Mark 1:11 belongs to a much earlier Christology called the 'adoptionist Christology' (because God 'adopted' Yeshua as His Son at the time of his baptism). The adoptionist Christology likely represents the oldest tradition about Yeshua as Messiah (Christ). In the baptismal pericope this tradition may be traceable directly to Yeshua. We have already seen that the source of most of the details in the pericope must have been Yeshua himself, as otherwise we would never have known of them. Why not this detail also? Consider Yeshua's saying that one must be 'reborn from above' to enter the kingdom of God [Jn 3:3; 3:5-8]. Is it not plausible that Yeshua may have told his disciples he had been 'reborn from above' when the Spirit descended upon him? We believe this is what happened and that his description of the experience eventually led to the use of Psalm 2:7 as a proof-text of that experience.

Even more firmly, we believe the adoptionist Christology is both the most original and the most accurate theory of the nature of Yeshua as Messiah. For example, this Christology explains why we know practically nothing about Yeshua's life before his baptism by John. There is essentially nothing to be known. Yeshua became Messiah at his baptism by virtue of having received what we call 'Christ consciousness.' Before that time, though he may have been exceptional, he was not unusual enough to have attracted much attention. Indeed, secular history knows almost nothing of him even as Messiah.

The word "adoptionist" is, however, a misnomer, an inaccurate description of what happened. One does not *beget* an adopted child, one begets a biological child. Rather than calling him an adopted son, the voice says that Yeshua has been reborn as God's own son: "today I have begotten you." Hence we rename this earliest Christology the "rebirth Christology," a distinction that will prove important later.

For these reasons we believe that the origin of Yeshua's Messianic consciousness can be traced to his baptismal experience at the hands of John. That experience, and its immediate aftermath, is expressed in the most reliable traditions as follows:

❑   John baptizes Yeshua;

❑   Yeshua experiences 'the heavens opening up' and the Spirit descending upon him;

❑   He has the experience of being reborn;

❑   He goes into the desert to 'sort things out'; and

❑   He is tempted by Satan.

The first of these is merely the triggering event. All the others are well-supported by the testimony of many of those who received Christ consciousness during their lives, as shown by Bucke. The three specific temptations reported by Matthew and Luke are also supported in Bucke. They are closely paralleled in the story of the Buddha who, immediately after his enlightenment, was tempted by the three daughters of Mara, the Evil One. The rebirth experience—the third point in the list above—is attested to by the proof-text from Psalm 2.7: "today I have begotten you": he has been begotten anew by the Spirit of God.

The tradition outlined above must, as we said, have come directly from Yeshua. If we might be so bold as to conjecture what it was that Yeshua actually may have told his disciples about his baptism and its aftermath, we might—putting it in more or less modern English—come up with something like this:

> I went down to the river Jordan where John baptized me. When I came up out of the water and opened my eyes, it was as though the heavens opened up before me, and I felt the Spirit of the Lord descending upon me. At that moment I became as one newly born from above. I couldn't remain among men, for as yet I knew not fully what had happened to me. So, at the bidding of the Spirit, I went into the wilderness, where I stayed for a long time. Satan tried to tempt me while I was there, but I rejected him. The Son of man comes not for his own glory, but for the glory of the Father.

We have Anglicized the names here. Speaking in Aramaic, Jordan is *Yarden*, and John is *Jochanan*.

As will become apparent as we delve more deeply into the life of Yeshua the Messiah, the term "Son of man" with which he referred to himself so often was evidently his term for Christ consciousness. In this respect, it was a name fully comparable to Whitman's "the other that I am," Dante's "Beatrice," and many others that we could enumerate, all used by those who enjoyed Christ consciousness to some degree.

The basis of Christianity

Many biblical scholars put the cart before the horse. Rather than treating the Resurrection as the signal event upon which a great religion was eventually to be constructed, they regard it as an ad hoc mechanism used to enhance the mass appeal of an existing religious movement. But in that case Christianity prior to formulation of the Resurrection 'myth' was based on . . . what? Thin air? Without the horse, the cart goes nowhere.

The fatal flaws in Christianity

If you want to find out what orthodox Christianity really believes you can do no better than to read Emil Brunner's *The Mediator*.[2] It has several strikes against it: It is out of print and hard to find.[3] Brunner is excessively wordy and very difficult to understand in places. He uses far too many untranslated foreign words and quotations. He uses too much space attacking Liberalism, Rationalism, Humanism, Philosophy, and Mysticism (you would do well to disregard anything he has to say about mysticism; his comments merely reveal his almost complete lack of understanding on the subject). The book has, however, one overriding advantage: it is the most knowledgeable treatment of orthodox Christian theology we have ever read. It cuts through the mythological trappings to the essential core of the Christian faith, and this core is much deeper and more realistic than one might suspect beforehand. We do not have the space here to adequately treat the subject, nor is it our task to do so. If you must know it in its entirety you will have to find the book and read it. We present here only a skeletal outline.

As Brunner sees it, Christianity is based on four cardinal points:

- ❑ **The Creation**, a beginning that qualifies the world (the universe) as divine;
- ❑ **The Fall**, Original Sin, which cuts the "bridge" between God and mankind;
- ❑ **Reconciliation**, or **Atonement**, which is the event of revelation in the coming of Christ and begins the process of restoring the broken "bridge"; and

❑   **Redemption**, signaled by the events of the Cross and the
     Resurrection, which completes the restoration of the broken "bridge"
     between God and mankind.

Brunner points out, correctly, that these four points "are indissolubly
connected with one another," and that they "form a unity," a unity
which "contains nothing that is irrelevant." In other words, if one
thing is removed the whole structure collapses. And collapse it
must, for there are some fatal flaws in this structure. It is like a chain
with weak links. The weakest link is the second point: the doctrine
of the Fall from innocence. Christianity states that man himself was
originally created wholly good, innocent and obedient to God, but
has since fallen from grace. By his own free will, given him by God,
man has turned against his Creator, rebelled against the divine authority of God. God's holiness will not allow Him to simply take man
back into His good graces; it demands a price. And man will not
mend the bridge himself—indeed, it is impossible for him to do so
for he cannot pay the price of his own redemption. It sounds like a
stalemate. Yet God wants to take man back. He is still the shepherd
who looks for the one lost sheep. So He sends us the Mediator,
Christ, who restores the bridge, paying Himself, on the Cross, the
price demanded by God's holiness. This, in a nutshell, is Christianity
according to Brunner.

All of this has been carefully thought out over a period of some
two thousand years by pious, intelligent persons. Yet there are some
fatal flaws in the argument, as we said. There is nothing wrong with
the first point above, the Creation. Indeed, science itself has discovered the event that Christianity calls "the Creation" and has fairly
well defined when it occurred and what happened afterwards. Science,
however, says nothing and can say nothing about how or why the
universe was created. The cause of the Creation necessarily lies
outside the universe, and there are no data about any such things.
They are beyond the domain of science.

But the second point, the Fall of mankind, we cannot agree with.
Yet it is not the fallen state of mankind we fault but rather the idea
that man was once thoroughly good. The fallen state of mankind

consists merely of the fact of sin, which is separation from God. No one today will seriously question that man is separated from God. How many people do you know who have a direct line to God? So it is not the present state of mankind but rather its preceding condition that is the issue here. We cannot accept the doctrine that man was once good. We do not believe that he ever occupied a state higher than the one in which he finds himself today.

For us, the doctrine of a divine Creation followed by a Fall presents a serious problem. First, we have an infinite, omniscient God who creates a wholly divine world for His own good and sufficient purposes. Then we are presented with the idea that this stupendous creation has run amuck, all because puny mankind has dared to stick out his tongue at his own Creator. Certainly the plans of man "*gang aft agley*," but are the plans of God similarly afflicted? Are we to imagine God is a poor designer who could create a divine world that promptly self-destructs? Is it possible that God 'created' the universe to produce self-aware life forms such as mankind without 'anticipating' that man would rebel against Him?

No, it is not possible. It is impossible that God would not have anticipated such a development. Indeed, it is impossible even that He would have had to do any such anticipating. God exists in eternity, which is another way of saying that He is constrained neither by space nor by time. It is just as correct to say God 'will create' the universe as it is to say He 'created' it. Probably the best way is to say that God 'creates' the universe. He did not have to 'look ahead' at the moment of creation to see that man would rebel. God can 'see' all of history, from the beginning to the end of the universe (if there is to be one), all at once. In other words, He 'would have seen' man's rebellion 'before' He created the universe. More precisely, *man's rebellion against God is implicit in the act of Creation.* It follows from this that God is ultimately responsible for having allowed man to run amuck. Why, then, should He demand such a high price for mending a break He 'always knew' was going to happen?

If we examine the story of the Fall as it is presented in the Bible [Gn 2:15-24] we make an interesting discovery. Man was thrown out of the Garden of Eden because he attained self awareness. By this we mean the state of consciousness, as described in Chapter 2. Man is the sole possessor of full-time self consciousness, or more precisely, self awareness. And only self awareness confers upon its possessors the power to distinguish between good and evil or the capacity to feel ashamed of one's nakedness. Yet these are the very things that the Genesis story uses to describe the Fall of man. Thus Adam and Eve are prototypes of the first self conscious human beings, not the first humanoids. So the answer to the question "Where did Cain's wife come from?" is that she was a simple-conscious woman, not self-aware. Of course the story is merely an allegory in any event.

Before man acquired self consciousness he existed in a state of simple consciousness like other animals. Thus it is true that he was in a state of innocence before the Fall. But is it also true that he was 'man' as we understand the term today? We think not. Self consciousness is essential to being fully human. A person can be defined as a self conscious human being. Those few humans who never achieve self consciousness are regarded as mentally limited. Therefore it would appear that the *Fall* was actually a *rise*. The moment we rose from simple to self consciousness we left behind innocence and became capable of knowing God.

These things God 'would have known' from the beginning. Unless we are to accuse God of incompetence—which seems very impudent to us—we must assume that these events were part of God's plan for the universe. In other words, He fully intended that we should rise from innocence and become vested with a will of our own (an ego). The Bible even says so. It states that God gave mankind a free will, an attribute of self conciousness. Why, then, should He require some great price to be paid on behalf of all humanity to restore a relationship between us that never existed?

Brunner states that the real damage of sin comprises the guilt that it engenders. What is done is done, and nothing we can do will ever erase the evil our sin has worked. The enormity of humanity's collective guilt requires no less than that the only begotten Son of God should suffer and die on the Cross to effect the Redemption. As Brunner correctly points out, this requires a unique once and for all event—the Revelation and Redemption through the Mediator—for its resolution. Here Christianity falls into the ultimate egocentric error we mentioned earlier. All of this might be true if what we do in this world is itself of ultimate significance, but it is not. This world is as nothing compared with the kingdom of God (or with heaven). Yeshua himself said as much: What does it profit a man to gain the world if he lose his life? Since we all die eventually, he must have meant something much greater by the term "lose his life."

Therefore what happens here is of only transient importance. We see from this that the only impediment between man and God is the individual's sinful ego. It is the ego that rebels against God. The collective guilt of humanity is only an illusion. This precludes the requirement that some great price must be paid as compensation for our collective guilt. The yawning gulf between man and God, to which Brunner often refers, exists to be sure. But it is a personal abyss between each person and God, not between humanity and God. Brunner is correct when he says that only the Mediator can bridge this gap, but He must come to each of us in person. A unique once and for all event is neither necessary nor sufficient.

Furthermore, if the 'Fall' comprises the acquisition of self consciousness by mankind we have an additional problem: infants are not born self conscious. No one knows exactly when self aware-ness is attained by growing children, but it apparently happens at some point during their first three years. This means that every child is born innocent, since a simple conscious being is incapable of rebellion against God. Thus a second monkey wrench falls into the works of Christian dogma, because this fact also denies the need for a humanity-wide redemption, which is the very doctrine of the Cross. It does, however, leave open the question whether a personal price may have to be paid. A price not to atone for some past sin that caused a separation between man and God but to establish a new bond between each person and God—a relationship that has never existed before.

We shall return to this subject later.

Notes

[1] Chilton, Bruce. *Rabbi Jesus: An Intimate Biography*. New York: Double-day (Random House), 2002. Pp. 12-15.

[2] Brunner, Heinrich Emil. 1947. *The Mediator: A Study of the Central Doctrine of the Christian Faith*. Translated by Olive Wyon. Copyright 1947 by W. L. Jenkins. Philadelphia: The Westminster Press.

[3] *The Mediator* has been reprinted. Cambridge, U.K.: James Clarke & Co., 2002.

～ ❀ ～

Chapter 4
The Son of Man

IN THIS CHAPTER WE EXPLORE HOW YESHUA perceived himself. Like others who have been endowed with Christ consciousness, Yeshua had his own name for the "other that he was" (to use Whitman's terminology). He called his higher self "the Son of man." There has been some controversy over just what phrase Yeshua actually used here. Chilton holds that it was "one like the person" (*Rabbi Jesus*, 2000). But it does not really matter what words Yeshua used or what they ordinarily meant in Aramaic. What does matter is that whatever the term Yeshua used, it meant his Christ consciousness, not his ordinary mortal self.

Having stated that, we shall now discuss how Yeshua used this phrase, which for the sake of continuity we shall continue to call "the Son of man." This is the term with which most people are familiar, and it is also the phrase that will come up repeatedly in the standard scriptural quotations of the things Yeshua said.

In examining the sayings of Yeshua in this chapter, as in the next also, we do not consider things that he said that did not concern his conception of himself. The Sermon on the Mount is beautifully poetic, but it sheds little light on how Yeshua saw himself or how he perceived the kingdom of God (which we treat in the next chapter). Likewise, we shall not consider the accounts of miracles and similar pericopes except as they might pertain to Yeshua's conception of himself.

An "interim" ethic?

In one of the passages making up the collection referred to as the Sermon on the Mount, which scholars have proclaimed to have been a number of separate sayings "sewn" together to form a cohesive whole, Yeshua reveals a radically new ethic. In Matthew 5:38-45 Yeshua says: "You have heard it was said 'An eye for an eye and a tooth for a tooth.' But I say to you, Do not resist an evil one. But if anyone strikes you on one cheek, turn to him the other; and if anyone would sue you and take your coat, let him have your cloak as well; and if anyone forces you to go one mile, go with him two miles. . . . You have heard it was said 'You shall love your neighbor and hate your enemy.' But I say to you, Love your enemies and pray for those who persecute you, so that you may be sons of your Father who is in heaven; for he makes his sun rise on the evil and on the good, and sends rain on the just and on the unjust."

This ethic is so radical that Albert Schweitzer (*The Quest of the Historical Jesus*) believed it was only an "interim ethic," meant to apply during the period between Yeshua's Resurrection and the coming of the kingdom of God. He was wrong. Yeshua was laying down a new and radical ethic that presupposes the kingdom of God and therefore reveals Yeshua's conception of his own person as the Son of man who saw things from a viewpoint totally different than that of ordinary people.

Mark, the first of the Gospels (erroneously placed second in the Christian canon, after Matthew), has few sayings directly mentioning the Son of man. He does, however, have a passage that describes a point of view that is attributable to Yeshua's Christ consciousness:

"Hear me, all of you, and understand: there is nothing outside a man which by going into him can defile him; but the
things that come out of a man are what defile him." And when
he had entered the house, and left the people, his disciples
asked him about the parable. [*Although it was not really a parable per se.*] And he said to them, "Then are you also without
understanding? Do you not see that whatever goes into a man
from outside cannot defile him, since it enters not his heart
but his stomach, and so passes on?" . . . "What comes out of a
man is what defiles a man. For from within, out of the heart of
man, come evil thoughts, fornication, theft, murder, adultery,
coveting, wickedness, deceit, licentiousness, envy, slander,
pride, foolishness. All these things come from within and they
defile a man." [Mk 7:14-23; Mt 15:16-20]

Notice here that Yeshua makes no reference to the results of these
evil thoughts. In this he shows evidence of Christ consciousness:
that there is no evil and no sin except in the mind of the perpetrator,
who is defiled.

The few passages containing the term "Son of man" in Mark are
in chapters nine and ten, and they are all sayings pertaining to the
suffering of the Son of man and include predictions of his crucifixion. Biblical scholars do not believe any of these sayings are genuine,
and they do not contribute to our understanding of the mind of
Yeshua in any pertinent manner.

A later pericope in Mark reveals Yeshua's understanding of the
world when some Sadducees ask him whose wife a woman would be
after resurrection if she had several husbands during her lifetime,
and Yeshua replies to them as follows:

"Is this not why you are wrong, that you know neither the scriptures nor the power of God? For when they rise from the dead, they
neither marry nor are given in marriage, but are like angels in heaven.
And as for the dead being raised, have you not read the book of
Moses, in the passage about the bush, how God said to him, 'I am
the God of Abraham, and the God of Isaac, and the God of Jacob'?
He is not the God of the dead, but of the living; you are quite
wrong." [Mk 11:24-27; cf. 1 Co 15:35-40; 42-44; 49-50]

In another short Markan pericope Yeshua is quoted as having
taught in the Temple, "How can the scribes say that the Christ
[Messiah] is the son of David? David himself, inspired by the Holy
Spirit, declared, 'The Lord said to my Lord, Sit at my right hand, till I
put your enemies under your feet.' David himself calls him Lord; so
how is he his son?" [Mk 12:35-37] Here Yeshua seems to deny that he is
descended from David and quotes scripture to uphold his position.

In another passage Yeshua states a theme that will become more
evident in the later Gospels: "If anyone says to you, 'Look, there is
the Christ!' or 'Look, there he is!' do not believe it." [Mk 13:21] He
said this because Christ consciousness comes from within a person;
Christ is not someone you recognize on the street.

Later in the same series of quotations (no doubt put together by
the author of Mark), Yeshua says, "Truly, I say to you, this generation will not pass away until all these things will take place. Heaven
and earth will pass away, but my words shall not pass away. But of
that day or that hour no one knows, not even the angels in heaven,
nor the Son, but only the Father." [Mk 13:30-32] Yeshua is clearly
denying that he can see the future, so predictions of his crucifixion
attributed to him are false. Precisely what he is referring to in the
first part of this passage is unclear. But if he is speaking of the coming of Christ consciousness—a big "if" in this case—the saying is
accurate enough. He does say that the universe ("heaven and earth")
will pass away, but Christ will not pass away.

Passing on to the second Gospel, that of Matthew, which was evidently written with a Jewish audience in mind, we find more sayings
of Yeshua attributed to the Son of man or displaying his Christ consciousness. For instance, one problematical saying, "Foxes have
holes, and birds of the air have nests, but the Son of man has
nowhere to lay his head," [Mt 8:20] can be attributed directly to
Yeshua's Christ consciousness: because it is a state of mind, it has
"nowhere to lay its head." Matthew chapter eleven, verse twenty-
seven gives as succinct a statement of Yeshua's Christ consciousness
as one will find anywhere: "All things have been delivered to me by
my Father; and no one knows the Son except the Father, and no one

knows the Father except the Son and anyone to whom the Son chooses to reveal him." We will see similar themes quoted later.

Another theme found in all three synoptic Gospels is this passage from Matthew: "While he was still speaking to the people, behold, his mother and brothers stood outside, asking to speak to him. But he replied to the man who told him, 'Who is my mother, and who are my brothers?' And stretching out this hand toward his disciples he said, 'Here are my mother and my brothers! For whoever does the will of my Father in heaven is my brother and sister, and mother.'" [Mt 48-50] This shows Yeshua's sense of identity with others.

These verses from Matthew are both decisive and deceptive:

> Now when Yeshua came into the district of Caesarea Philippi, he asked his disciples, "Who do men say that the Son of man is?" And they said, "Some say John the Baptist, others say Elijah, and others Jeremiah or one of the prophets." He said to them, "But who do you say I am?" Simon Peter replied, "You are the Christ, the Son of the living God." [Mt 16:13-16]

We have already said that this reply by Peter is not credible. The idea that Yeshua was the Son of God had not even been conceived of at that time; it would be more than one hundred years before that became part of the church kerygma. In the rest of the text, Yeshua goes on to say that he is making Peter the foundation of his church. But scholars are agreed that Yeshua never intended to found a church; that was a much later development. It is quite obvious that many of these words have been put into the mouth of Yeshua in order to lay the foundation for later church doctrine. If there is any truth to this passage, Peter must have said, "You are the Messiah." Anything more is window-dressing by the church.

A critical pericope is related in Matthew chapter sixteen: "[25]For whoever would save his life will lose it, and whoever loses his life for my sake will find it. [26]For what will it profit a man, if he gains the whole world and forfeits his life? Or what shall a man give in return for his life? [27]For the Son of man is to come with his angels in the glory of his Father, and then he will repay every man for what he has done. [28]Truly, I say to you, there are some standing here who will not taste death before they see the Son of man coming in his king-dom." [Mt 16:25-28] Verse twenty-seven may be a redaction either by the author of Matthew or by later church scribes; it does not fit well with the rest of the quotation. But all of us lose our lives eventu-ally, so Yeshua must have meant a much greater thing by "forfeits his life." Verse twenty-eight is doubtless a prediction that some of those Yeshua was addressing would attain Christ consciousness before dying a natural death.

Matthew adds the following to the material quoted by Mark [Mk 13:21]: ""So if they say to you, 'Lo, he is in the wilderness,' do not go out; if they say 'Lo, he is in the inner rooms,' do not believe it. For as the lightning comes from the east and shines as far as the west, so will be the coming of the Son of man." [Mt 24:26-27] Since this quo-tation appears only in Matthew and Luke, it must derive from Q (for *Quelle*, German for 'source'), a manuscript that once contained many sayings of Yeshua but has been lost to history. This saying fits well with what is known of the coming of Christ consciousness. It is like a sudden flash of lightning that lights up the world and reveals to the person attaining it the true nature of reality: the kingdom of God. Luke has the wording as "For as the lightning flashes and lights up the sky from one side to the other...." [Lk 17:24]

Matthew also "fudges" wording used later by Luke, who writes that Yeshua said, "Why do you call me good? No one is good but God alone." [Lk 18:19]; Matthew has this as "Why do you ask me about what is good? One there is who is good." [Mt 19:17] Matthew makes this saying ambiguous; Luke is direct and to the point.

Earlier in Matthew there is the saying that Jimmy Carter made famous: "You have heard it was said, 'You shall not commit adultery.' But I say to you that everyone who looks at a woman lustfully has already committed adultery with her in his heart." [Mt 5:27-28] What is significant about this pronouncement is that Yeshua is say-ing thinking is as important as doing. This complements the saying that what goes into a person is not important, it is what comes out—what the person is thinking. These ideas will prove valuable in defining the kingdom of God as Yeshua saw it.

Another saying that also appears in Matthew [11:18-19] is given by Luke as: "For John the Baptist has come eating no bread and drinking no wine; and you say, 'He has a demon.' The Son of man has come eating and drinking; and you say, 'Behold, a glutton and a drunkard, a friend of tax collectors and sinners!' Yet wisdom is justified by all her children." [Lk 7:33-25] Yeshua apparently is referring to Christ consciousness by saying "wisdom is justified by all her children."

Luke contains much the same saying as Matthew [16:25-28], but with Matthew's verse twenty-seven rather significantly different: "For whoever would save his life will lose it; and whoever loses his life for my sake, he will save it. For what does it profit a man if he gains the whole world and loses or forfeits himself. For whoever is ashamed of me and of my words, of him will the Son of man be ashamed when he comes in his glory and the glory of the Father and of the holy angels. But I tell you truly, there are some standing here who will not taste death before they see the kingdom of God." [Lk 9:24-27] The close similarity of the first two verses and the last between Matthew and Luke suggests they come from a common source. The third line is quite different in Luke and in Matthew. We suspect the true kernel of this verse is in the words "Whoever is ashamed of me and of my words, of him will the Son of man be ashamed. . . ." and that the words "when he comes in his glory and the glory of the Father and of the holy angels" are a redaction to presuppose agreement with the later church doctrine about Yeshua as the supernatural Christ.

Again, the same theme as given in Matthew [11:27] appears in Luke: "All things have been delivered to me by my Father; and no one knows who the Son is except the Father, or who the Father is except the Son and anyone to whom the Son chooses to reveal him." [Lk 10:22] This same theme will be amplified in the Gospel of John later on.

In chapter eleven of Luke he depicts accurately the relationship between Jonah and Yeshua: "This generation is an evil generation; it seeks a sign, but no sign shall be given to it except the sign of Jonah. For as Jonah became a sign to the men of Nineveh, so will the Son of man be to this generation. The queen of the South will arise at the judgment with the men of this generation and condemn them; for she came from the ends of the earth to hear the wisdom of Solomon, and behold, something greater than Solomon is here. The men of Nineveh will arise at the judgment with this generation and condemn it; for they repented at the preaching of Jonah, and behold, something greater than Jonah is here." [Lk 11:29-32] Thus, the sign of Jonah has nothing to do with his having been in the belly of the fish for three days and three nights, but rather in his successful call to the men of Nineveh to repent.

The *Interpreter's Bible* tells us the "the queen of the South" is a reference to the notorious Queen of Sheba. It adds that Mark [8:12*b*] probably left out the words "Except the sign of Jonah" because he didn't understand it and adds "But it is much more likely that [Yeshua] himself was thinking of the message of repentance. . . ." Few experts today believe that Yeshua predicted his own demise. It is unlikely that Yeshua was referring to himself by the words "something greater than Jonah is here." This undoubtedly refers to the kingdom of God. Before John's baptism of Yeshua, the Jews had only the word of the Law; now they have the kingdom of God—if they could just see it.

A brief passage in Luke [19:10] has Yeshua saying that "the Son of man came to seek and save the lost." This may represent Bucke's finding that those possessing Christ consciousness believe they have the power to pass this consciousness on to others.

In a post-resurrection speech attributed to Yeshua, he says, "Thus it is written, that the Christ should suffer and *on the third day* rise from the dead, and that repentance and forgiveness of sins should be preached in his name to all nations, beginning from Jerusalem." [Lk 24:46*b*-47] This has the stamp of the later church all over it, but the significant words—in italics above—are "on the third day." This same phrase is used in many places in the Gospels and negates the idea of Yeshua's entombment lasting "three days and three nights." which is so ingrained in current church thinking. In fact, the period of his confinement between burial and the discovery of the empty tomb was a mere thirty-six hours—exactly half that of a period of three days and three nights, which comprises seventy-two hours.

From above or again? [Jn 3:3-8]

This pericope presents a problem in translation similar to that posed by Luke 17:21 (see Chapter 5). The pertinent part is the conversation between Yeshua and Nicodemus in John 3:3-8:

> ³Yeshua answered [Nicodemus]: "I say to you truly, unless one is born from above, he cannot see the kingdom of God." ⁴Nicodemus said to him, "How can a man be born when he is old? Can he enter a second time into his mother's womb and be born?" ⁵Yeshua answered, "I say to you truly, unless one is born of water and the Spirit, he cannot enter the kingdom of God. ⁶That which is born of the flesh is flesh, and that which is born of the Spirit is spirit. ⁷Do not marvel that I said to you, 'You must be born again.' ⁸The wind blows where it will, and you hear the sound of it, but you know not whence it comes or where it goes; so it is with every one who is born of the Spirit."

The same Greek word, *anothen* (ανοθεν), is here translated as 'from above' in 3:3 and as 'again' in 3:7. This word has three different meanings in Greek: 'from above,' 'again,' and 'for a long time' (past). It is used 13 times in the New Testament, ten times with the first meaning, twice with the second, and once with the third. It seems plain from the context, however, that the author wishes us to understand both 'from above' and 'again' as the meaning here. After Yeshua states that one cannot see the kingdom of God unless he has been "born from above," Nicodemus asks (and it is irrelevant here whether Nicodemus actually spoke these words or not) how a person can be reborn. Evidently the author wants to make it plain that both meanings are intended. He has Nicodemus ask a question that shows he (Nicodemus) understood 'again' as the meaning of *anothen*. Therefore, in Yeshua's reply we have translated *anothen* as 'again,' since it is for this meaning of the word that Yeshua has replied to Nicodemus. In the last verse above, the same word means both 'wind' and 'spirit,' again demonstrating the Semitic penchant for puns. After all, why use two words when one word can be made to do double duty?

Summing this up, to be reborn from above—"born of the Spirit"—means that Christ consciousness dawns within you, as Luke says [17:21]. Then, and only then, can you "see the kingdom of God" or "enter the kingdom of God." The sense in which one both sees and enters the kingdom through the process of spiritual rebirth becomes plain when we consider that with the awakening of Christ consciousness one is able to see that he is in the kingdom and so has entered into it. Otherwise, the sense would have to be purely physical: that the kingdom of God is a particular place one can enter into. But in that case it would be possible to say, "There it is." And Yeshua said this is impossible.

More sayings about the Son of man in John

A fascinating passage from John describes how Yeshua sees the relationship between himself as Christ and God: "Yeshua said to them, "Truly, truly, I say to you, the Son can do nothing of his own accord, but only what he sees the Father doing; for whatever he does, that the Son does likewise. For the Father loves the Son, and shows him all that he himself is doing. . . . [Jn 5:19-20] Interpreted, Yeshua is apparently saying that he sees his Christ consciousness as the reflection of God (i.e., your reflection in a mirror can do only what you do, and anything you do it must do likewise or the reflection would not be true to life). As you might expect, the traditional interpretation of these words by ecclesiastical authorities is much less mystical than ours. But Christ is nothing if not mystical. The actual term "Son of man" does not appear in these verses, but is implied, as shown by a subsequent verse [Jn 5:26-27]: "For as the Father has life in himself, so he has granted the Son also to have life in himself, and has given him authority to execute judgment, because he is the Son of man."

John picks up this idea later in a number of passages. "For this is the will of my Father, that everyone who sees the Son and believes in him should have eternal life; and I will raise him up at the last day." [Jn 6:40] The Interpreter's Bible says that the refrain "I will raise him up at the last day" has appeared to be inconsistent with the

Johannine doctrine of eternal life. As is often true, the interpretation is too literal. Perhaps Yeshua means the time of a person's death by "the last day." The last day of everyone's life is the moment of death. This may be the "last day" to which Yeshua refers here.

John goes on to elaborate on this issue:

> Yeshua answered them, "Do not murmur among your-selves. No one can come to me unless the Father who sent me draws him; and I will raise him up at the last day. It is written in the prophets, 'And they shall all be taught by God.' Everyone who has heard and learned from the Father comes to me. Not that anyone has seen the Father except him who is from God; he has seen the Father. Truly, truly, I say to you, he who believes has eternal life. I am the bread of life." [Jn 6:43-48]

Several verses later John has Yeshua saying "Truly, truly, I say to you, unless you eat the flesh of the Son of man and drink his blood, you have no life in you; he who eats my flesh and drinks my blood has eternal life, and I will raise him up at the last day. For my flesh is food indeed, and my blood is drink indeed. He who eats my flesh and drinks my blood abides in me, and I in him." [Jn 6:53b-56] Aside from John's activism for the Eucharist, which is understandable, the important words here are "abides in me, and I in him." Participation in the Eucharist was believed to confer Christ consciousness upon true believers. Sadly, this is not true.

As John Robinson eloquently put it in his controversial book *Honest to God*, [Yeshua] "emptied himself utterly of himself," thus denying any self-consciousness, so that God and only God could show through. We cannot think of a more succinct description of Christ consciousness. And John writes: "I and the Father are one" [Jn 10:30] and "The Father is in me and I am in the Father." [Jn 10:38]

In the famous Transfiguration event on a high mountain reported by Mark [9:2-8], Matthew [17:1-8], and Luke [9:28-36] Yeshua appeared as a dazzling white figure (doubtless somewhat of an exag-geration) to three of his disciples. Whereas Wilson (*ibid.*) suggests that this episode may been nothing more than a hypnotic suggestion, Bucke clearly shows that this sort of thing is sometimes reported of others who possessed Christ consciousness in some degree, and he points out that the haloes often used to depict very spiritual humans doubtless derive from this phenomenon.

Wilson's folly

Ian Wilson's book *Jesus: The Evidence* (New York, Harper & Row, 1984) is well-written, thorough, fully documented, and a most interesting read. It becomes problematical when Wilson seeks to explain the source of Yeshua's apparent charisma and powers as evidence that he used hypnosis and possibly post-hypnotic suggestions to work apparent miracles, including his own resurrection following the Crucifixion. Poor Ian! He has fallen into the same trap as have so many before him: no sooner do they attempt to penetrate into the mind of Christ than they trip over their own folly.

It is human nature to be suspicious of anything one cannot see for oneself. Why else would Yeshua have said, "Blessed are those who believe without seeing"? This phenomenon is a dangerous thing. Humans seem programmed to find a rational explanation for things that happen. This is only natural. There are no doubt "rational" explanations for everything we discuss in this book. Remember the dictum: "There are no miracles, only things we do not yet understand."

Richard M. Bucke was probably the first, and possibly one of the very few human beings, to understand the workings of Christ consciousness. This was most likely because he himself had experienced a brief glimpse of it. That the power and charisma of one such as Yeshua could be attributable merely to a state of consciousness seems incredible. Yet it is true.

Mark well our words here: Never—**never!**—dismiss something as impossible simply because you haven't experienced or cannot know it yourself. It is not given to all of us to have the mind of Christ.

Back to the Gospel of John

Having thus briefly digressed, let us return to further examination of the evidence beginning with the sixth chapter of the Gospel according to John. Here Yeshua says, "Do you take offense at this? Then what if you were to see the Son man ascending where he was before? It is the spirit that gives life, the flesh is of no avail; the words that I have spoken to you are spirit and life. But there are some of you who do not believe." [Jn 6:61-64] Again, he is evidently speaking of the Christ consciousness—the spirit and life—that allows him to see the immanent kingdom of God. A bit later, Yeshua emphasizes this same point: "My teaching is not mine, but his who sent me; if any man's will is to do his will, he shall know whether the teaching is from God or whether I am speaking on my own authority. He who speaks on his own authority seeks his own glory; but he who seeks the glory of him who sent him is true, and in him there is no falsehood." [Jn 7:16-19] In other words, if another should attain the same vision of the kingdom as Yeshua, he would realize that Yeshua speaks the truth.

Now we come to one of the hardest sayings of Yeshua, from chapter 14 of John: "I am the way, and the truth, and the life; no one comes to the Father but by me. If you had known me, you would have known my Father also; henceforth you know him and have seen him." [Jn 14:6-7] Many have doubted that Yeshua would actually have made such a statement. But it is undeniably true. Christians' mistake has been to identify the "I" in this statement with the human being called Yeshua of Nazareth. But here Yeshua is clearly referring to Christ consciousness, for that is the only way out of this universe and therefore "to the Father." To know this Christ (as opposed to the merely human Yeshua) is to know God, and thus know the Father.

Yeshua emphasizes this difference later in the same chapter of John, saying: "If a man loves me, he will keep my word, and my Father will love him, and we will come to him and make our home with him. He who does not love me does not keep my words; and the word which you hear is not mine but the Father's who sent me." [Jn 14:23-24] Could he have said this any more plainly? "We will come to him and make our home with him": Christ consciousness will come to him and live within him. And his words are "not mine but the Father's who sent" him: It is the Christ consciousness that speaks these words, not the human Yeshua.

It may seem to you, the reader, that we are belaboring this point. But we believe it cannot be overemphasized. It comprises the root and meaning of the entire story of Yeshua, the Son of man.

In the verses following those quoted just above, John goes on to give a voice to Yeshua that in some respects echoes the position of the later church: "These things I have spoken to you, while I am still with you. But the Counselor, the Holy Spirit, whom the Father will send in my name, he will teach you all things, and bring to your remembrance all that I have said to you." [Jn 14: 25-26] We have no doubt that the Holy Spirit here is—or was in Yeshua's original wording—Christ consciousness, which comes from God, the Father. The words "while I am still with you" may be an addition by the author of John, who, like the authors of the other Gospels is continually stressing the theme that Yeshua knew he was going to die. It was important to the church to establish this, since otherwise Yeshua's nature as a divine being would be compromised.

In the stories related about Yeshua's appearance before various governmental or religious officials, such as Pontius Pilatus, Praefectus of Yudea, and Herod Antipas, as well as the chief priest of the Sanhedrin, Caiaphas, Yeshua is reported to have stated "You have no power over me" or words to that effect. He was, of course, speaking of his nature as Christ, not as the merely human Yeshua. These mortals would have had no more power over the divine Christ consciousness than they would have had over the course of the sun or moon.

An interesting insight into Yeshua's consciousness comes from words he reportedly said while dying on the cross. Mark gives the words in Aramaic: "*Eloi, Eloi, lama sabachthani?*" which he translates as "My God, my God, why have you forsaken me?" [Mk. 15:34] Matthew gives the first words in Hebrew, "*Eli, Eli, lama sabachthani?*" which mean the same thing. Perhaps Matthew wished to make the name more like that of Elijah, whom onlookers took as Yeshua calling on to save him. Neither Luke nor John reports these words; Luke substitutes "Father, into your hands I commit my spirit!" [Lk 23:46] All three authors state that the words were spoken at "the sixth hour." John says that Yeshua merely said, "It is finished!" and gave up his spirit.

Certainly it makes sense that these words would be gradually altered or omitted entirely in later Gospels, as they detract from the assumed divinity of Yeshua.

Non-canonical sources on the Son of man

The *Gospel of Peter*, long known by reference and fragments of which were discovered in 1884, also has the passion narrative. In this 'lost' gospel, the words of Yeshua on the cross are reported to have been, "My power, my power, why have you forsaken me?" This makes more sense than the canonical versions. We think it perfectly understandable that such an exalted state as Christ consciousness would be difficult if not impossible to maintain under the almost indescribable agony of dying by crucifixion. The words "my power" could very well refer to Yeshua's Christ consciousness, which had left him during his death agonies.

The so-called Coptic *Gospel of Thomas*, one of the papyri found in the Nag Hamadi hoard in 1945, dates back to the late fourth or early fifth century AD but is based on a primitive text that must have been produced in Greek about 140 AD, which itself was based on even more ancient sources. So this text is of an age comparable to that of the canonical Gospels themselves. It is not a true gospel but a collection of *logia* (sayings), many of which can be found in similar or nearly identical form in the canonical texts. Only a few of the logia reveal anything direct about the consciousness of Yeshua, but those that do are of the utmost interest here.

Logion 77 reads: "Yeshua said: I am the Light that is above them all, I am the All, the All came forth from Me and the All attained to Me. Cleave a [piece of] wood, I am there; lift up the stone and you will find Me there." This speaks clearly of Christ consciousness and shows how Yeshua saw it as pervading reality.

Logion 106 reads: "Yeshua said: When you make the two one, you shall become Sons of man, and when you say: 'Mountain, be moved,' it will be moved." Clearly, the latter half of this logion reflects the canonical texts on the subject of moving mountains. The words "make the two one" must refer to the merging of the mind of a human being with the consciousness of Christ, making the two as one.

Logion 108 reads: "Yeshua said: Whoever drinks from My mouth shall become as I am and I myself will become he, and the hidden things shall be revealed to him." Once again, we have the concept of the merging of Yeshua's Christ consciousness with the mind of another person ("I myself will become he"). The hidden things would, of course, comprise the kingdom of God.

The Gospel of Mary of Magdala

We come now to a most excellent book by renowned biblical scholar Karen L. King: *The Gospel of Mary of Magdala: Jesus and the First Woman Apostle* (Santa Rosa, California: Polebridge Press, 2003). This fragmentary text was written sometime in the early second century AD and lost for more than 1,500 years. Introducing it, Dr. King writes: "This astonishingly brief narrative presents a radical interpretation of [Yeshua's] teachings as a path to inner spiritual knowledge; it rejects his suffering and death as the path to eternal life; it exposes the erroneous view that Mary of Magdala was a prostitute for what it is—a piece of theological fiction; …." [page 3] In Chapter 6, titled "The Son of Man," Dr. King writes in part:

> In the *Gospel of Mary* the "Son of Man" is the child of true Humanity, the Image of the Divine Realm that exists within every person. It is identified as the true Image of nature to which the disciples are supposed to conform, the image of humanity's true spiritual nature. In his farewell to the disciples, the Savior tells them: "The child of true Humanity exists within you" (4:5). The savior commands them: "Follow it! Those who search for it will find it" (4:6).
>
> . . .
>
> Note how one is *not* to find it: by looking outside of oneself. The *Gospel of Mark*, for example, understands the Son of Man to be a messianic figure who will come in clouds with power and glory in the end times (13:26). In contrast, the *Gospel of Mary* admonishes: "Be on your guard so that no one deceives you by saying, 'Look over here!' or 'Look over there!'" This warning shows a knowledge of apocalyptic eschatology, such as we see in the *Gospel of Mark* and many other sources, but it

rejects it entirely. The *Gospel of Mary* does not understand "Son of Man" as a messianic title and never uses it to refer to [Yeshua]. For the *Gospel of Mary*, it refers to the ideal, the truly human.

—*Gospel of Mary of Magdala*, pp. 59-60

We would add to this simply that the *Gospel of Mary* refers to the title Son of man as Christ consciousness, the full development, or perfection, of the human condition.

The mystery behind the term "Son of man"

Yeshua was not original in using the term "Son of man" itself, yet it was odd that he consistently used this term to refer to himself. The Greek for "Son of man" is ὁ υἱὸς τοῦ ἀνθρώπου, literally "the son of man." Although the word "son" is usually capitalized as "Son" in the New Testament, and often the word "man" itself, these forms are not found in the Greek versions. They are editorial redactions by the various translators of the Bible.

Bruce Chilton's assertion that the term should be translated as "the one like a person" (*Rabbi Jesus*, page 158) need not be taken seriously. Chilton adds: "He is called the 'one like a person' (which can also be translated as 'son of man') because he has a human face." (*Ibid.*) There are two instances of "son of man" in Daniel, and in the Book of Ezekiel there are no less than ninety-three occurrences of the term. There is little doubt, however, that most if not all of these references are to a messianic figure. Daniel writes in Chapter Eight, verses thirteen and fourteen: "I saw in the night visions, and behold, with the clouds of heaven there came one like a son of man, and he came to the Ancient of Days [*i.e., God*] and was presented before him. And to him was given dominions and glory and kingdom, that all peoples, nations, and languages should serve him; his dominion is an everlasting dominion, which shall not pass away, and his kingdom one that shall not be destroyed." (RSV)

That Yeshua used the term "Son of man" to refer to himself can hardly be imagined other than as a claim to messianic authority. Yet, keeping in mind our earlier dictum to 'think Hebrew' when studying biblical texts dating back some two thousand years, we should stop to realize that the Jewish penchant for double meanings may come into play here. One notices the extensive use of parallel constructions in these ancient texts, where the same thing is said over again in slightly different words.

In our view Yeshua's use of the term "Son of man" to refer to himself carried such a double meaning. For instance, he insisted that one could not see the kingdom of God unless he were born anew, or born from above. Now, in the case of a male person, who is it that is born? A son, of course. We believe that Yeshua used "Son of man" to refer to his reborn self, born "of water and the Spirit." His internal "Son of man" refers to his Christ consciousness and is thus comparable to Dante's "Beatrice" or Walt Whitman's "the other that I am." It is no wonder that the Son of man "has no place to lay his head": he is Christ consciousness, a mode of thinking, which obviously would have no need of a place of rest. Yeshua was "yanking the chains" of his disciples when he made that complaint.

Even such an exalted being as Yeshua of Nazareth was not immune to the desire for a bit of humor.

Summary

In this chapter we have reviewed the sayings (and a few actions) of Yeshua that reveal his own consciousness of his mission and his nature as Messiah, or Christ. In virtually every example the characteristics of Christ consciousness, as depicted by Richard Bucke in his book *Cosmic Consciousness*, have been exemplified. In these sayings, Yeshua reveals himself as the Son of man, which is evidently his term for the Christ consciousness that came over him upon his baptism by John. He explicitly states that the Son of man can do nothing on his own accord but "only what he sees the Father doing," and therefore he is a reflection of the glory of God the Father. We have found not a single instance of such a saying of Yeshua that does not accord with this theory of his consciousness. There remains now only the task of examining those sayings and actions of Yeshua that reveal his conception of what he called "the kingdom of God" to see if they, too, conform to this new theory of the mind and evident consciousness of Yeshua.

Judea and Galilee at the time of Yeshua

This map shows the locations of most of the places mentioned in the text. We have added the Galilean Bethlehem to the original map. Note the spelling of Judea on the map title—the ancient spelling "Iudea."

Chapter 5
The Kingdom of God

WE NOW TURN TO HOW YESHUA PERCEIVED THE KINGDOM OF GOD. Yeshua often refers to the kingdom of God in his sayings, but not always in a way that defines what he means. Sometimes he describes it merely as someplace that is very desirable to attain. This aspect we are not concerned with; rather we are interested in what he means by the kingdom of God.

A place one can find?

If there is anything definitive about what Yeshua says about the kingdom of God it is that it is not a place one can find by going about looking for it. There is not much in Mark, the first Gospel, to indicate what Yeshua meant by the kingdom of God. A hint, probably more extensive originally, is found in chapter four: "With what can we compare the kingdom of God, or what parable shall we use for it? It is like a grain of mustard seed, which, when sown upon the ground is the smallest of all the seeds on earth; yet when it is sown it grows up and becomes the greatest of all shrubs, and puts forth large branches, so that the birds of the air can make nests in its shade." [Mk 4:30-32] Here Mark has taken what is probably an original saying of Yeshua's and made it into some kind of prediction of the growth of the church, something Yeshua himself never would have done. The original may have been an allegory of the sudden appearance of the world as the kingdom of God as revealed by the expansion of his consciousness from a "tiny seed" into a glorious vision encompassing all of nature (the "birds of the air").

When his disciples rebuked him for mixing with little children, Yeshua said, "Let the children come to me, do not hinder them; for to such belongs the kingdom of God. Truly, I say to you, whoever does not receive the kingdom of God like a child shall not enter it." [Mk 10:14-15] Little children are innocent and see the world differently than do adults; Yeshua says they are closer to the kingdom of God than those who see through worldly eyes.

Matthew has much more to say about the kingdom, which he usually terms the "kingdom of heaven" (preferring not to use the name of God as do the other evangelists); he writes that as soon as Yeshua returned from the desert he began to preach, "Repent, for the kingdom of heaven is at hand." [Mt 3:17] Note that Yeshua does not say the kingdom is coming: it is "at hand." It is immanent, right here and now, but men do not see it.

Later, Yeshua makes a definite pronouncement about this kingdom: "Truly, I say to you, among those born of women there has risen no one greater than John the Baptist; yet he who is least in the kingdom of heaven is greater than he. From the days of John the Baptist until now the kingdom of heaven has suffered violence and men of violence take it by force." [Mt 11:11-12] Among mortal men, none is greater than John the Baptist, but John does not have Christ consciousness. Thus he who has the least of Christ consciousness is greater than John. Yeshua sees the world as the kingdom of God (heaven), and he has seen it thus since he was baptized by John. When Yeshua sees the world—and therefore the kingdom of God—

being done violence by violent men, he recognizes this and so tells his disciples. There are probably few words in the Bible that are more misunderstood than those in this passage.

In the parable of the leavened bread [Mt 13:33] Yeshua likens the kingdom of heaven to leaven, a hidden ingredient that changes the entire nature of the loaves of bread that it leavens.

Passing on to the book of Luke, we find Yeshua saying, "The law and the prophets were until John; since then the good news of the kingdom of God is preached, and everyone enters it violently." [Lk 16:16] The Interpreter's Bible comments about this: "One of several sayings in the gospel tradition that speak of the new age of God's rule as a fact of present experience, not just an event of the last days." (8:288) Exactly. But this is not really a "new age" of God's rule; it is simply that God's rule has been revealed as the truth behind the world of appearances, a revelation enabled by Yeshua's Christ consciousness. He preaches this to whomever will listen.

Among you or within you?

Considerable controversy has arisen over the translation of Luke 17:21. This is the second verse of a two-verse pericope:

> Being asked by the Pharisees when the kingdom of God was coming, he answered them, "The kingdom of God does not come in an observable way; nor will they say, 'Lo, here it is!' or 'There!' for behold, the kingdom of God is among you."

A footnote to the last two words reads, Or: "within you." The word in question is *entos* (εντοσ), 'middle,' which is derived from the root *en* (εν), meaning 'in' or 'inside.' The root ωεσοσ, *en*, is used 70 times in the New Testament, twice with the meaning of 'among'—in Rm 12:3 and 1 Co 14:25. Two other words are used to mean "among" in the New Testament. The word *mesos* (μεσοσ—among, in the midst, in the middle, surrounded) is used 59 times, 17 times with the meaning 'among.' The word *pros* (προσ) plus an accusative (ωιτη, in the presence of) is used seven times, twice with the meaning 'among.' The word *entos* is used only once with the alleged meaning 'among'—in Lk 17:21. It is used twice in the New Testament, the other occurrence being in Mt 23:26, where it is used in the phrase "first clean the inside of the cup." Here the meaning intended by the word *entos* is quite clear: it means 'inside' or 'within,' not 'among.' If the writer of Lk 17:21 meant to write 'among' or 'in the midst of' (so the RSV), why did he not use *en*, or *mesos*, either of which can plainly mean 'among'? Why would he have gone out of his way to use a word whose meaning might not be obvious in the context?

We believe the fault lies with the translators and not with the author of Luke. It is plain to us that they wish to see the kingdom of God placed within Yeshua himself and not inside the Pharisees. But that is not what Yeshua meant anyway. He meant that the kingdom of God comes from within a person, not from the outside. Thus, it can be neither observed coming—it does not come in an observable way—nor seen 'here' or 'there,' as Yeshua said. We think this is the only intelligent way the pericope can be translated and understood. The meaning 'within' is obviously in accord with our theory of Christ consciousness, and it also agrees with the words of Yeshua reported by the author of John in the pericope about Nicodemus [Jn 3:1-21].

This is the most important pericope in the New Testament concerning the kingdom of God. The author of the book of John does not mention the kingdom of God directly, and thus little more can be learned from the canonical texts about this kingdom.

Non-canonical texts, however, add a great deal that is important to understanding what Yeshua meant by the kingdom of God. The *Gospel of Thomas* starts right out with Logion 3: "Yeshua said: If those who lead you say to you: 'See, the Kingdom is in heaven,' then the birds of heaven will precede you. If they say to you: 'It is in the sea,' then the fish will precede you. But the Kingdom is within you and it is without you. If you know yourselves, then you will be known and you will know that you are the sons of the Living Father. But if you do not know yourselves, then you are in poverty and you are poverty."

Again, "Yeshua said: Blessed is he who was before he came into being. If you become disciples to Me and hear My words, these stones will minister to you." [Thom Log. 19] The kingdom of God pervades everything.

And here we see an echo of the canonical gospels: "Yeshua said: From Adam until John the Baptist there is among those who are born of women none higher than John the Baptist, so that his eye will not be broken. But I have said that whoever among you becomes as a child shall know the Kingdom, and he shall become higher than John." [Thom. Log. 46] An intriguing twist on the other versions.

"His disciples said to Him: When will the repose of the dead come about and when will the new world come? He said to them: What you expect has come, but you know it not." [Thom. Log. 51] Obviously, the subject here is the kingdom of God. Yeshua says that it is already here, but his disciples do not know it.

"His disciples said to Him: When will the Kingdom come? Yeshua said: It will not come by expectation; they will not say: 'See, here,' or 'See, there,' but the Kingdom of the Father is spread upon the earth and men do not see it." [Thom. Log. 113] This is one of the most important sayings of Yeshua about the kingdom of God. It echoes some of the canonical gospels but adds that the kingdom of God "is spread upon the earth" yet men do not see it. This stresses the immanence of the kingdom of God. Yeshua can see it because he has Christ consciousness, but others cannot see it because their eyes have not been opened. The canonical versions leave out this part, probably because it conflicts with the church doctrine of the coming kingdom of God, which will arrive at the end days. The church cannot countenance sayings that dispute this teaching.

Those who cover their ears cannot hear.

The kingdom of God as ineffable

The word *ineffable* has two rather distinct meanings. The first meaning is "incapable of being expressed in words." The second meaning is "unspeakable," including things that are taboo. Richard Bucke in his book *Cosmic Consciousness* emphasizes that much of what persons who attain Christ consciousness see and learn is ineffable, in the sense that it cannot be expressed in our everyday language. This is doubtless the reason Yeshua described the kingdom of God mostly in parables, parables that shed little light on what the kingdom of

God really was. It was certainly valuable beyond measure—the "pearl of great price"—yet it could not be put into words that an ordinary person could understand.

Such a state of affairs would seem to be beyond description for most of us. There are, however, parallels we can draw that give some insight to what is meant by ineffable here. (We shall return to the second meaning later, only to point out that it is merely an escape mechanism for those who do not understand.)

First, imagine a world unlike our own. One that is relatively flat with only small hills here or there, and with a climate that is equable throughout from pole to pole. Rainfall is limited to local showers that pop up at random, and temperatures lower than say, 59 degrees Fahrenheit (15 degrees Celsius) are unknown anywhere. Now imagine that you are speaking to some of the inhabitants of this strange world. How would you describe snow? How would you describe glaciers? Mountain ranges like the Himalayas? These people would have no words to describe things of this sort, because there would be no need for them. You would find these concepts to be ineffable to these people. You know perfectly well what snow and glaciers are, but you would be utterly unable to describe them to people without any concept of such things.

Going even farther afield, how would you describe a rainbow to a blind person? Without any concept of color, the names of the colors of the rainbow would be meaningless to this sightless person. Your frustration would be total in such an endeavor.

These examples give but a feeble representation of what it would be like for one with Christ consciousness to try to describe what the kingdom of God looks like to an ordinary person.

GETTING BACK TO THE SECOND MEANING of ineffable, here is the Apostle Paul's account of what is clearly an episode (or perhaps two episodes) of Christ consciousness that he experienced sometime around 44 AD:

> I know a man in Christ who fourteen years ago was caught
> up to the third heaven—whether in the body or out of the
> body I do not know, God knows. And I know this man was

> caught up into Paradise—whether in the body or out of the
> body I do not know, God knows—and he heard things that
> cannot be told, which man may not utter. [2 Cor 12:2-4]

The Greek words used here can mean either incapable of being expressed in words or unspeakable, taboo. Most interpreters— including both *The Interpreter's Bible* and Bruce Chilton in his book *Rabbi Paul*—choose the latter meaning. It is incomprehensible to them that Paul could have meant that the things he saw could not be expressed in words. But we believe that is precisely what he meant. That he could have meant something so simple as the concept that all who are in Christ are Israelites by conversion (Chilton) is unreal.

Certainly the notion that all who have the indwelling Christ could be considered as Israelites was radical for the time. But one would hardly need to be transported to Paradise to come up with an idea like that.

There are none so blind as those who will not see.

Albert Schweitzer in his seminal work *The Mysticism of Paul the Apostle* (New York: The Seabury Press, 1968) does not address the meaning of the Greek word translated as ineffable by us. He does, however, hit the nail squarely on its head when he says Paul's "great achievement was to grasp, as the thing essential to being a Christian, the experience of union with Christ." (page 377)

Why the kingdom of God is so hard to define

Surprisingly few of Yeshua's sayings directly address the question of what the kingdom of God is. He does say that the kingdom is already here. Yeshua, as the Son of man (Christ) sees this kingdom. He tells others that this kingdom of God is both within them and without them. The best translation of the Greek word *entos* (εντοσ) in Luke 17:21 is probably "pervades": the kingdom of God pervades you. You are in it, it is part of you, and you are part of it.

This was Yeshua's chief obstacle in preaching his good news of the kingdom of God. He was faced with the almost insurmountable task of describing that which only he, as the Son of man, could see and describing it in terms that his disciples and followers could under-stand. Sadly, he never quite succeeded in this heroic task. Or if he did, the words he used were so misunderstood by his listeners that they were not passed on in the oral tradition that preceded the written texts, and so were lost to us.

In a very few instances, some of these words were passed on to us, but not in the canonical texts, only in non-canonical sources that were regarded as heretical by the early church. It is easy to dismiss that which one does not understand as "heresy" and relegate it to the junk heap of history. Here are a few choice examples from the *Gospel of Thomas.*

Logion 1: "And He said: Whoever finds the explanation of these words will not taste death. (2) Yeshua said: Let him who seeks, not cease seeking until he finds, and when he finds, he will be troubled, and when he has been troubled, he will marvel and he will reign over the All."

Such a one will be troubled because what he finds will disrupt everything that he thought he knew about this world. But when he has come to terms with this troubling information, he will marvel at what he has found and become like the Son of man.

The last portion of Logion 3 reads: "If you [will] know yourselves, then you will be known and you will know that you are the sons of the Living Father. But if you do not know yourselves, then you are in poverty and you are poverty." Recall the Biblical meaning of "know" which can mean a merging of bodies (sexual knowledge of a woman by a man) or souls. The "know yourself" then means to merge with the Son of man, whom the Father sends. If you do that, then you will know that you are a son of the Living Father.

Logion 5: Yeshua said: Know what is in your sight, and what is hidden from you will be revealed to you. For there is nothing hidden which will not be manifest.

Logion 17: Yeshua said: I will give you what eye has not seen and what ear has not heard and what hand has not touched and [what] has not arisen in the heart of man.

Logia 18-19: The disciples said to Yeshua: Tell us how our end will be. Yeshua said: Have you then discovered the beginning so that you inquire about the end? Blessed is he who shall stand at the beginning, and he shall know the end and he shall not taste death. Yeshua said: Blessed is he who was before he came into being. If you become disciples to Me and hear My words, these stones will minister to you.

Logion 22: Yeshua saw children who were being suckled. He said to his disciples: These children who are being suckled are like those who enter the Kingdom. They said to Him: Shall we then, being children, enter the Kingdom? Yeshua said to them: When you make the two one, and when you make the inner as the outer and the outer as the inner and the above as the below, and when you make the male and the female into a single one, so that the male will not be male and the female [not] be female, when you make eyes in the place of an eye, and a hand in the place of hand, and a foot in the place of a foot, [and] and [an] image in the place of an image, then you shall enter [the Kingdom].

This is one of the most difficult passages in Thomas. Undoubtedly Yeshua's words were so esoteric that some of them have been lost in the oral tradition that preceded the writing of the Gospel of Thomas. It is very hard to make sense out of what Yeshua says here, yet one is haunted by the feeling that there is some hidden meaning in these words, a meaning that dances around on the fringes of consciousness without ever coming into the light of meaning. It is like trying to recall a word, a word that almost comes to you time and time again, but which never quite surfaces in your conscious mind. Perhaps someday. . . .

Logion 37: His disciples said: When will You be revealed to us and when will we see You? Yeshua said: When you take off your clothing without being ashamed, and take your clothes and put them under your feet as the little children and tread on them, then [shall you behold] the Son of the Living [One] and you shall not fear.

Logion 51: His disciples said to Him: When will the repose of the dead come about and when will the new world come? He said to them: What you expect has come, but you know it not.

Clearly, Yeshua is saying that the Kingdom is already here.

THE OBTUSENESS OF MOST OF THESE SAYINGS should be sufficient to demonstrate the difficulties inherent in describing the kingdom of God. Many great minds have struggled with this problem, mostly without any real success. Some things that Christ consciousness reveals are diametrically opposed to the teachings of the Christian church—for example, that the ultimate good of all beings is assured, or that sin has no reality except in the mind of the sinner. Frankly, concepts such as these must have been redacted from any genuine sayings of Yeshua that may have been passed down in the early oral tradition. Such revisions would have been our principle of potential exclusion in savage action.

The Apostle Paul's take on the kingdom of God

It may seem strange to be discussing Paul in a book about Yeshua. Yet there are two good reasons for doing so: First, Paul himself was a recipient of Christ consciousness; and second, he spent a great deal of time and words trying to describe the kingdom of God himself.

Paul's Christ consciousness was not as complete or as forceful as that of Yeshua, but he had his own contributions to make on the subject. His well-known conversion while on the road to Damascus has striking parallels to other cases of Christ consciousness. His use of the phrase "the scales fell from my eyes" sounds very much like the description of someone who is seeing something for the first time, something that was there all along but which the "scales" over his eyes prevented him from seeing. His ensuing sojourn to Arabia—which then was even a more desolate place than it is today—is comparable to Yeshua's "forty days and forty nights" (a Semitic colloquialism meaning a fairly long time) in the wilderness. Such retreats are typical of those receiving Christ consciousness for the first time.

Paul believed that the act of baptism instilled Christ's spirit in an individual. It certainly had when Yeshua was baptized, and even though Paul's own baptism by Ananias had been after the fact, so to speak, he felt it was also true of himself. He was not bashful about asserting this, writing "For I through the law died to the law, that I might live to God. I have been crucified with Christ who lives in me; and the life I now live in the flesh I live by faith in the Son of God, who loved me and gave himself for me." [Gal 2:19-20] He repeats this shortly afterward, writing "For in Christ Yeshua you are all sons of God, through faith. For as many of you were baptized into Christ have put on Christ." [Gal 3:26-27] And again, he writes that "because you are sons, God has sent the Spirit of his Son into our hearts, crying, 'Abba! Father!' So through God you are no longer a slave but a son, and if a son then an heir." [Gal 4:6-7]

In his first letter to the Corinthians, Paul writes, "Yet among the mature we do impart wisdom, although it is not a wisdom of this age or of the rulers of his age, who are doomed to pass away. But we impart a secret and hidden wisdom of God, which God decreed before the ages for our glorification. None of the rulers of this age understood this; for if they had, they would not have crucified the Lord of glory. But, as it is written, 'What no eye has seen, nor ear heard, nor the heart of man conceived, what God has prepared for those who love him,' God had revealed to us through the Spirit. For the Spirit searches everything, even the depths of God." [1 Cor 2:6-10]

Bruce Chilton in *Rabbi Paul* (New York: Image Books / Doubleday, 2004) writes: "To 'live by the faith of God's son' involved being in a relationship with God that was so close, it meant more than understanding God or believing in God. By the force as suffusion of Spirit, the *core of one's being became divine in a transformation whose meaning was infinite, beyond the capacity of the human mind to grasp.*" [page 180; emphasis added] Here Chilton asserts the very thing that he denies in other places.

In other words, this transformation was ineffable, just as Paul himself had written of his own experience. He had been transported to the "third heaven" or "Paradise" where he saw and heard things that were impossible to put into words. And this included the kingdom of God, for as Paul writes, ". . . the kingdom of God does not consist in talk but in power." [1 Cor 4:20]

Chilton (*ibid.*) believes that what was "unutterable" about Paul's experience related in his second letter to the Corinthians (ca 56 AD) was that being baptized into Christ made one into a "son of Abraham." But if this was so, why then did he pronounce as "unutterable" that which he had already been preaching and practicing for a number of years (Ga 4:7 ca 50 AD) before writing that letter? Surely, Paul meant a great deal more than such an earthly, if controversial, position.

Like Yeshua, Paul had difficulty in defining exactly what he meant by the "kingdom of God."

The kingdom of God in the early church

The descriptions that have come down to us about the way the early Christians lived—indeed, even before they were called "Christians"—seem almost marvelous. Although few, if any, of these early Christians, received the special consciousness that blessed Yeshua, they seem to have been determined to practice what he had preached to his disciples and followers. They have even been described as the "first communists," living in communities where share and share alike was a reality. Some of the descriptions of them that were made by outsiders reflect a sense of awe at the nature of these early practitioners of the Christian faith.

The Apostle Paul is credited with having made Christianity a mainstream religion even though his principle belief was that having the mind of Christ was what made a person a Christian. Beginning in the early second century AD, men of secular bent set about constructing a church that suited their purposes—which seem to have been manipulating believers and creating a strict organization to promulgate rules and regulations that would keep members in line.

The Christian church was finally torn asunder from its roots by the emperor Constantine at the Council of Nicaea in 325 AD. The distortion of Yeshua's message into something he never would have recognized was then complete; the church would never be the same again. Its core message was lost in the mists of history. Yet it can be discerned even today: distorted, but not completely forgotten. We have attempted to resurrect this original meaning here.

The Nicene Creed held that Yeshua was divine, the third person of the Trinity: God, the Son, and the Holy Spirit. All of this because Yeshua of Nazareth possessed a special consciousness that revealed his Father: the Creator and His creation. He could truly be called "the man who knew too much."

Let those who have eyes with which to read understand.

≈ ≈

Summary

In contrast with the phrase "Son of man," which appears in numerous places in the Old Testament, the term "kingdom of God" (βασιλεία [ν] τοῦ θεοῦ) appears only in the New Testament. The similar term "kingdom of heaven" (βασιλεία[ν] τῶν οὐρανῶν) appears only in Matthew, who, writing for a Jewish audience, did not want to spell out the name of God (although it slipped through in five places in his Gospel). The latter term appears in Matthew 31 times, in three forms. Mark uses the "kingdom of God" in 15 places; Matthew uses it in only five places (which may be the result of a scribe or editor having inserted these apparently authentic verses into Matthew without realizing how careful the author of that Gospel had been to avoid using the term); Luke uses it in 32 places; John uses it just twice; and it appears in Acts seven times. In addition the term appears in First Corinthians four times, and once each in Romans (14:17), Galatians (5:21), Colossians (4:11), and Second Thessalonians (5:1). Altogether, there are 101 places in the New Testament where either "kingdom of God" or "kingdom of heaven" is used. The vast majority of these are not descriptive of this kingdom except to declare how valuable it is (e.g., the pearl of great price) or the lengths to which one should go to obtain it (e.g., the man who sells everything to purchase the field where buried treasure lies). We have discussed in this chapter the pericopes wherein there is some description, no matter how indirect, of what the kingdom of God comprises.

Regardless of the paucity of these results, it should be apparent that Yeshua was the author of the term "kingdom of God," since it appears nowhere in any of the Old Testament books. Our conclusion that the kingdom of God represented Yeshua's term for the world as seen through the eyes of Christ seems virtually inescapable.

In a sense it is unfortunate that Yeshua saw his Christ consciousness as having been the direct result of his baptism by John. That this is true is evidenced by verses such as John 3:5, where Yeshua states that "unless one is born of water and the Spirit, he cannot enter the kingdom God." Clearly, the "water" is a reference to baptism. The act of baptism became a central tenet of the theology of the Apostle Paul, and has become deeply embedded in the theology of the Christian church. In fact, for hundreds of years the death of a child before baptism was considered a major tragedy by millions of Christians around the world. We believe, however, that Yeshua's baptism by John was simply a trigger for the release of the latent Christ consciousness that had been lying dormant within his mind for some time before that.

We have no way of knowing whether or not Yeshua believed that his baptism by John was the cause of his Christ consciousness, but if he did, he was surely not the only person ever to have confused cause and effect.

～ ✿ ～

Chapter 6
The Resurrection Experience

THE RESURRECTION IS CENTRAL TO THE CHRISTIAN FAITH. It has been truly said that without the Resurrection experience there would be no such thing as Christianity. But what really happened when Yeshua was apparently resurrected? Was this event truly contrary to the laws of nature and therefore some kind of miracle? How are we to explain this extraordinary—if only alleged—occurrence?

Some great persons throughout history—St. Augustine and Baruch Spinoza among them—have said that there are no such things as miracles, only things that we do not yet understand. We believe the Resurrection is one of those things we do not understand—yet. An experience that happened to one of the authors (David) in the spring of 1973 is an actual event of this kind.

The Broken Bottle

ONE FINE SPRING SUNDAY in 1973, five days after the sudden death of my paternal grandmother—a dear, sweet lady whom I loved greatly—I found myself wandering into a woods adjoining a park in

Rockville, Maryland. While walking along an unfamiliar path, soothing my sense of loss with the beauty of the woodlands in the spring sunshine, I became aware of a presence. Sensing somehow that it was my grandmother, I called out her name in my mind. She answered that it was, indeed, her. Not knowing what else to do, I thought, "How are you?" Immediately she replied, "Perfectly marvelous! Why, I don't even need my glasses any more, and I can see everything just ever so clearly!"

There was no doubt in my mind that those were precisely the words my grandmother would have used. Still, I was not sure of what I was experiencing; could it be just my own overwrought imagination? Then I walked on, not caring what the answer was but just delighting in the experience. After we had thus communed in silence for some time, I decided to retrace my way to the park. In a short while I came to an unfamiliar fork in the path. After a brief deliberation as to which way I had come, I chose the right-hand path. But almost as soon as I began to walk I sensed that something was wrong. Then I heard my grandmother's voice in my mind:

"David! You've taken the wrong path. Look under that tree!"

I looked under a large juniper tree on my right. There I saw the remains of one of those common dark green pop bottles—a thousand bits and pieces of glass flashing green fire in the afternoon sun. She was right. I had passed numerous deposits of trash and debris of one sort or another on my way into the woods, but this nearly star-shaped array of green glass fragments was most certainly not one of them. Quickly I retraced my steps to the fork and took the left-hand path. Within a few minutes I was back in the park. The short walk home passed uneventfully.

That evening I told my wife, Retta, about my experience in the woods. I was hesitant to tell her, unsure myself whether the episode had been real or imaginary. My doubts were to be short-lived. The next weekend I took Retta to see the place where my experience had taken place. As we walked along the path into the woods, I saw the same piles of debris I remembered seeing the week before: beer cans, magazines, newspapers—all the careless droppings of humanity that seem an incorrigible part of the American way of life. When we came to the fork where I had taken the wrong turn before, I took Retta to see the broken bottle my grandmother had pointed out to me. In a few yards we came to the spot. Sure enough, there was the big juniper tree. But when I started to point out the broken bottle, I went numb with shock. It was gone!

Thinking that surely someone had cleaned it up, I kneeled down and pawed frantically through the dead leaves and juniper needles on the ground looking for pieces of the broken glass. There was none; the broken bottle had vanished without a trace. I knew with an awful certainty that there was no one within ten thousand miles of that place who would have taken the time and effort to pick up every one of those thousands of shards of glass. This was especially true since all the rest of the endless litter surrounding the spot had been left apparently undisturbed. And even if someone had cleaned it up, surely there would have been a few shards left to betray the earlier presence of the entire broken bottle. There was not a single one.

Gradually the awesome truth dawned on me: The bottle had never been there. My grandmother—probably tapping some of the power of the Christ consciousness with which she was doubtless already making contact—had caused me to see a broken bottle where none existed. But why? Did some terrible fate await me down that path, or was it merely that I might have gotten lost? To find out, we followed the other path and, within a hundred yards or less, came out in the same park from which we had started. This "wrong" path turned out to be shorter and more direct than the one I had originally followed.

It was then that I realized the true meaning of the broken bottle: It was my grandmother's way of satisfying a modern doubting Thomas. The words of Yeshua echoed in my mind: "Unless you see signs and wonders, you will not believe." [Jn 4:48]

I had seen a sign and now I believed.

The Resurrection

IT WAS NOT, HOWEVER, until three years had passed that I came to realize the full significance of the broken bottle that never was. My grandmother was a dear, sweet, kind, and forgiving soul, but she was not a saint. Even less so was she a Buddha or a Christ, and she herself would have been the first to say so. If, after being gone for five days, she could cause me to see a broken bottle where there was only leaf-strewn ground, what then could such a one as Yeshua cause people to see when he had been gone only two days?

Make no mistake about it: The broken bottle I saw was as real as anything I have ever seen in my life. I do not doubt for one instant that had I bent down to touch the broken glass it would have felt just as real as it looked. Nor do I doubt that it could have cut my finger and left a wound just as real as any I have ever suffered. No, that bottle was not just an illusion or some sort of hallucination. It was there, it was real. Nevertheless, as soon as I had left the spot it no doubt simply disappeared—if, indeed, anyone else could have seen it at all. I know this is paradoxical, but I also know it is true, even as I know that I live and breathe as I write these words. And it is precisely this paradoxical nature of the broken bottle that forms the key to understanding the resurrection of Yeshua.

The appearances

Let us now consider the resurrection appearances of Yeshua with a view towards the similarities between my experience of the broken bottle and the appearance of Yeshua to his friends and disciples. First, the man Yeshua died on the cross and was buried. The problem of the empty tomb does not concern us here. We must not "look for the living among the dead" [Lk 24:5]. That is a problem for those who seek the historical Yeshua. But it is not the historical Yeshua who saves: it is Christ who saves.

The self-aware Yeshua "died" when he was reborn as the Christ, most likely just after being baptized by John. Thus, to be precise we should say that it was the body of the man Yeshua that died on the cross. It was Christ who was "resurrected"—and even this is wrong because Christ cannot die; Christ is eternal. The Christ is the Being of cosmic consciousness, the Self, the Buddha: God. And God is beyond time. He is eternal.

Certainly it is within the power of Christ to appear to people as Yeshua if my humble grandmother could cause me to see a broken bottle. Let us then examine how Christ, as Yeshua, appeared to his disciples after the crucifixion.

The first to see Yeshua after the crucifixion were Miriam of Magdala and Miriam, the mother of James. The story appears in all four gospels, but only John gives the full details, and in John only Miriam of Magdala is involved. John recounts that "she turned around and saw Yeshua standing, but she did not know it was Yeshua," and supposed him to be the gardener [Jn 20:14-15]. Then he was seen by two of his disciples on the road to Emmaus as recorded by both Mark and Luke. Only Luke gives the details, writing "But their eyes were kept from recognizing him" [Lk 24:16].

Christ's next appearance was in Jerusalem, this time in easily recognizable form. Only Luke records it, writing "But [the disciples] were startled and frightened and supposed that they saw a spirit," and later "still disbelieved for joy and wondered" [Lk 24:37,41]. Finally, Luke states,"While he blessed them, he parted from them, and was carried up into heaven" [Lk 24:51].

John reports that Yeshua appeared twice to the disciples while they were still in Jerusalem, apparently in quite recognizable form. But of the first incident he writes cryptically, "… he showed them his hands and his side. *Then* the disciples were glad when they saw the Lord" [Jn 20:20; emphasis added]. The second incident, which John states took place eight days later, is the now-famous "doubting Thomas" episode. Here John writes, "The doors were shut, but Yeshua came and stood among them. . . ." [Jn 21:4]. In the first incident John implies that the disciples did not recognize Yeshua until he showed them the wounds in his hands and side. In the second, he appears suddenly inside a closed room.

Next, John records that Yeshua appeared to the disciples on the shore of the Sea of Tiberias (Sea of Galilee, or Lake Kinneret). He writes, "yet the disciples did not know that it was Yeshua" [Jn 21:4]. And after the point at which the disciple John (whose own disciple, in turn, was evidently the author of this gospel) had recognized him as Christ, the writer makes the strange comment that ". . . none of the disciples dared ask him, 'Who are you?' They knew it was the Lord" [Jn 21:12]. If it was obvious he was Yeshua, why would any of the disciples even have thought of asking who he was?

The last appearance of Yeshua recorded in the gospels (according to the most accepted chronology) was his appearance on a mountain in Galilee, reported by Matthew. He writes, "And when they saw him they worshipped him; but some doubted" [Mt 28:17].

The significance of these quotations for our present inquiry is in how Yeshua appeared to Miriam and the disciples, not in what happened. In the first two appearances Yeshua was not immediately recognized, nor is any mention made of wounds. These two may have been other persons whom Christ caused to be perceived and heard as Yeshua. We do not mean to imply possession; those persons were probably quite unaware of what happened. Whether these cases of initial nonrecognition, or partial recognition, were owing to design or to defects in execution we shall never know, and it does not concern us.

In the later episodes Yeshua seems to have been more easily recognized, although some still doubt or disbelieve and often there are some who apparently did not see him clearly. No doubt there is some connection between the faith of the viewer and the resemblance of the figure to Yeshua. How much easier it is to believe in a broken bottle on the ground than in a resurrected Yeshua!

Nevertheless, we must admit that this resurrected Yeshua did not possess a body made of the same mundane materials as ours. In Yeshua's second appearance, after breaking bread with the disciples (the person who may originally have been caused to look like him would have simply continued down the road) "he vanished out of their sight" [Lk 24:31]. In his third appearance he parted from the disciples and "was carried up into heaven" [Lk 24:51]. In the doubting Thomas episode of John, Yeshua materializes inside a room with closed doors.

Please do not misunderstand us. We are not saying that in His resurrection appearances Christ did not have a real body. That body was just as real as any of us have ever seen or touched, yet it was not subject to those inexorable laws of physics that our bodies must obey. It was the body of Christ having the appearance of Yeshua, not the mortal body of Yeshua. Thus it was not a human body subject to death and decay but a heavenly body, immortal and eternal.

Paul understood this and tried to tell us in these words:

> But some will ask, "How are the dead raised? With what kind of body do they come?" These are ignorant questions. What is sown does not come to life unless it first dies. And what is sown is not the body which is going to come, but a bare seed, perhaps of wheat or some other grain. But God gives it such a body as He has chosen, and to each kind of seed its own sort of body. For not all flesh is alike: there is human flesh, animal flesh, bird flesh, and the flesh of fish. There are heavenly bodies and earthly bodies, but the glory of the heavenly is one thing, and the glory of the earthly is another. . . .
>
> So it is with the resurrection of the dead: what is sown is perishable, what is raised is imperishable. What is sown is pitiful, but it is raised in glory. It is sown in weakness, it is raised in power. It is sown a physical body, it is raised a spiritual body. If there is a physical body, there is also a spiritual body. . . . And we, who have born the image of the earthly man, shall also bear the image of the man of heaven. I tell you this brethren: flesh and blood cannot inherit the kingdom of God, nor can the perishable inherit what is eternal. [From RSV: 1 Co 15:35-40; 42-44; 49-50; you should read these passages in several translations to discern their true meaning, and even then you may need the help of the Spirit.]

Paul does not say you cannot receive the kingdom of God while still in the flesh. He says that your flesh and blood body cannot itself inherit the kingdom. In other words, the coming of the kingdom of God—by which Paul means receiving the mind of Christ, the dawning of Christ consciousness—confers immortality on the soul, not the physical body. It does so by transforming the soul (Greek:

psyche: that which gives natural life, the self, whence *psychikon* = physical body) into the Spirit (Greek: *pneuma*: that which gives spiritual life; whence *pneumatikon* = spiritual body). Bruce Chilton writes (in *Rabbi Paul*, New York: Image Books / Doubleday, 2004), "When Paul thought of a person, he conceived of a body as composed of flesh, a physical substance that varies from one created thing to another (people, animals, birds, fish). But in addition to being physical bodies, people are also what Paul called 'psychic bodies,' by which he meant bodies with souls. Unfortunately, most modern versions of the Bible mistranslate this phrase. They distort Paul's language by having him speak of a 'natural' or 'physical body'; his own word at this point [1 Cor 15:44] is [*psychikon*] an adjective derived directly from the noun for 'soul' [*psyche*]. Bodies for Paul are not just lumps of flesh: *they are self-aware or self-conscious.* That self awareness is precisely what makes them 'psychic.'" [emphasis added] Note that Chilton points out the self aware nature of humans.

At the same time Paul is giving a clue to an even greater truth where he writes "*nor* can the perishable inherit what is eternal" [emphasis added]. In other words, the soul or "self" (*pysche*), which is mortal, cannot inherit the kingdom of God, which is eternal, without first becoming the Spirit (*pneuma*), which is itself eternal.

This is the essential prerequisite. The person who dies with only the self dies an unfertilized seed that cannot grow. But the person who dies with Christ's Self ("falls asleep in Christ," in Paul's words) dies as a seed made fertile by union with God (in Christ) and will grow into—become a part of, as it were—the Self of Christ, which is the (only begotten) Son of God. The self must be 'recycled,' but the Self is mature and passes on.

Becoming the greater Self, however, means giving up the smaller self. You must abandon your ego before you can receive the full knowledge of your union with God in Christ. Then and only then will it be not you, but "Christ who lives in you" [Ga 2:20].

Those who stubbornly cling to the expectation of literal bodily resurrection are but thinly disguising the wish to preserve their egos, their selves. Yet this is precisely what Yeshua and Paul tell us repeatedly we cannot do. We are not to put stock in possessions, reputations, or even friends and loved ones. In fact we must even hate our own lives, our own selves (read: egos), before we can enter the kingdom of God. Then we must take up a cross that symbolizes both the responsibility for and the love of all mankind if we are to follow him (Christ). Yet we cannot do any of these things for ourselves; we cannot do them with the ego but only in Christ.

And to inherit the Self of Christ, to realize our birthright of union with God, we must give up our egos, our selves—sacrifice them to God the Father.

There is no other way.

And so it was because of a lowly broken bottle and the love of a dear departed soul that I, David, first learned the greatest secret of life: the Way into the kingdom of God.

AND HERE WE MUST LEAVE YOU, dear reader. No matter how hard it may be to accept things like this, there is nothing like "seeing is believing," which is likely why Yeshua said "Blessed are those who believe without seeing."

Deus veritas est

The timing of the Resurrection

Many scholars have written extensively about the timing of the crucifixion of Yeshua based on the Last Supper having been a Passover meal. But other experts have pointed out that there is no real evidence that this was the case. If it were true, Yeshua would have been crucified either on a Wednesday or a Thursday, depending on which of two Jewish calendars was being used at the time. This is all irrelevant. The actual timing is pinned down quite neatly by the canonical scriptures themselves. They all agree that the crucifixion took place on "Preparation Day": the day before Passover, which happened to be on a *Shabbat*, the Jewish Sabbath, which is always on a Saturday.

(See Mk 15:42-45; Mt 27:57,58; Lk 23:50-52; and Jn 19:38a) In particular, John writes: "Since it was the day of Preparation, in order to prevent the bodies from remaining on the cross on the Sabbath (for that Sabbath was a high day), the Jews asked Pilatus that their legs might by broken, and that they might be taken away." [Jn 19:31] That Shabbat was a "high day" because it was also the Passover. This made it even holier than usual, and almost nothing could be done on such a day except prayer and worship.

Other authors have attempted to reconcile the timing of these events with the tradition that the preceding Sunday was "Palm Sunday." The timing then becomes difficult to resolve. The events now celebrated as Palm Sunday did not, however, occur around the time of Passover. From the description of those events, including the spreading of branches on the path around the temple, it seemed clear to us that what was being celebrated here was *Sukkoth*, not Passover or the feast of unleavened bread. Sukkoth, the Feast of Booths, or Feast of Tabernacles, is held in the fall, not in the spring when Passover is celebrated. This makes it months removed from the events of the passion and therefore totally disconnected from them. This belief is supported by no less an authority than Bruce Chilton, who writes in *Rabbi Jesus*: "As [Yeshua] and his group passed under the arch of the city's gate, they were swept up by the festive parade of other pilgrims on their way to the Temple. The morning sun glowed pink on the white stone of the city's buildings. The air was crisp and clean. Throngs of people waved willow branches and palm fronds, with lemons and sprigs of myrtle tied to them, all for the Sukkoth celebration of fertility. They marched and danced along, singing psalms and giving praise to the Lord. Many pilgrims unconnected with his movement had heard of [Yeshua] and felt a sense of joy and anticipation as they fell in with his company. They even commandeered an ass for [Yeshua] (Matthew 21:1-9; Mark 11:1-10; Luke 19:28-38; John 12:12-16), fired with the prospect of what this Sukkoth sacrifice could mean." [see pages 226-227, Image Books edition]

Therefore, the crucifixion took place on a Friday, now celebrated as "Good Friday." The body of Yeshua had to be buried quickly, and the texts relate that Joseph of Aramithea, a member of the Sanhedrin, offered a newly hewn tomb to hold the body. (John adds that another rabbi, Nicodemus, helped in the preparations [Jn 19:38-42].) There was not enough time for the women—and in those days it was "woman's work"—to prepare the body properly, washing and anointing it, so the body was hastily wrapped in a linen cloth and put into the tomb. The stories of Roman soldiers guarding the tomb because the Jews persuaded Pontius Pilatus that there was a plot by Yeshua's disciples to steal the body are errant nonsense. No Roman magistrate would have believed such a thing; neither would "the Jews" have had any reason to believe that Yeshua's followers might steal his body, Yeshua's "predictions" of his own crucifixion and resurrection being redactions by authors of the late first or second centuries AD. This story was concocted to strengthen the resurrection accounts.

We firmly believe that the Shroud of Turin is the same linen cloth that was used to wrap the body of Yeshua when it was placed in the tomb. We also predict history will prove us right and that ultimately the Shroud will be proved to be genuine.

But the women could not return the next day to finish the burial work because it was both the Jewish *Shabbat* and Passover, a holy day on which no work of any kind could be performed by a devout Jew. So the women went back near dawn on Sunday morning to finish the preparation of Yeshua's body for final interment, only to find the tomb empty.

Only one thing prevented the women from returning to Yeshua's tomb the following day to finish the burial preparations: the next day was a high holy day—a *Shabbat* Passover. Therefore the timing of the death, burial, and resurrection events is cast in concrete. There is no other viable solution.

When was the Crucifixion?

Much work has been done in an effort to determine when Yeshua was crucified. Aside from the impossible task of reconciling the triumphal entry in Jerusalem with Palm Sunday, which we have seen is fraught with many difficulties, various considerations place the most likely date of the crucifixion as 14 Nisan in the year 30 AD. This makes Yeshua the Paschal lamb, which was sacrificed at "dusk" on 14 Nisan, the beginning of the feast of unleavened bread. The following day, 15 Nisan, was a *Shabbat* and a high holy day because it was part of the Passover celebration. Nothing could be done then, so the women had to wait to finish the anointing and preparation of Yeshua's body for burial until 16 Nisan, a Sunday—"the first day of the week"—according to several of the Gospels. This was also the day of "first fruits," as stated by Paul [Rom 8:23; 1 Co 15:23], who repeatedly stresses that the risen Yeshua is the "first fruits" of the new Passover.

A possible alternative date, 33 AD, is ruled out by the stoning of Stephen, which is reported by several authors as having occurred as early as 32 AD (cf., Chilton, *Rabbi Paul*, p. 43). Stephen's martyrdom must have happened later than the crucifixion of Yeshua.

Interestingly, if this timing is correct, and if the length of Yeshua's ministry was only about one year (rather than the three years John reports), and if he was actually "about thirty years old" when he began to preach, then his birth date must have been very close to the year one, either BC or AD, and the fixing of the calendar by Dionysius Exiguus in 525 AD was rather close to the mark, rather than being seriously in error as has so long been assumed. Those assumptions were based on canonical texts, which were perforce guesswork when it came to the birth of Yeshua, since virtually nothing is known of him prior to his baptism by John ca 29 AD.

How many days?

In various of the canonical texts one finds two things mentioned: that Yeshua would rise on "the third day" and that he was in the tomb for three days (or three days and three nights) before the Resurrection. These accounts are irreconcilable. In the first century AD there was no concept of zero, which was invented around 500 AD in India; its use spread through the Arabic world eventually making its way into Western culture around 1200 AD. Thus there could be no day "zero" from which to count days after an event.

At the time of Yeshua, people had a simpler way of reckoning the time between two events. The day something happened was the "first day." The following day was the "second day," and the day after that, the "third day." Starting from a Friday, Sunday would be the third day, when the empty tomb was discovered. Thus, far from having been buried for "three days and three nights" before his empty tomb was discovered, Yeshua was interred for at most two nights (Friday night and Saturday night) and one day (Saturday). The Bible accounts of it having been three days and three nights derive from the story of Jonah (Jon 1:17): "And the Lord appointed a great fish to swallow up Jonah; and Jonah was in the belly of the fish three days and three nights." While Mark, the first Gospel, states only that Yeshua said "no sign shall be given to this generation" [Mk 8:12], Matthew and Luke both have Yeshua saying "The only sign [this generation] will be given is the sign of Jonah" [Mt 12:39; Lk 11:29]. Matthew adds to Yeshua's words, "For as Jonah was in the belly of the sea-monster for three days and three nights, so will the Son of Man be in the heart of the earth for three days and three nights." [Mt 12:40] John apparently knows nothing of this tradition.

If Yeshua did say that the only sign to be given was the "sign of Jonah"—which could easily have been true—he meant Jonah's call for repentance [cf. Lk 11:30-32]. Many scholars have pronounced it unthinkable that Yeshua could have predicted his own crucifixion. Christ consciousness does not confer the ability to see the future.

Why is this, and with what can we compare it? It is like a little boy who peers at a baseball game through a hole in the fence. He can see the players and the scoreboard, and after a while he can figure out what they are doing and why they are doing it. But he cannot discern who will win or what the final score will be until the end of the game.

Matthew evidently misunderstood Yeshua's remark that only the sign of Jonah would be given and managed to work the quote from the book of Jonah into a proof-text of the resurrection story. Sadly, his timing was off by a factor of two. Also, the time of the actual resurrection is unknown. It could easily have been within hours or even minutes of the time his body was left in the tomb.

Apologists have said that Matthew's "three days and three nights" was only meant as an approximation to the length of Yeshua's interment prior to the discovery of the empty tomb. Regrettably, this 'approximation' has become enshrined in the lore of Christianity and is even the viewpoint of church officials. Sad, because the real timing is revealed in the holy scriptures themselves in a form so simple that anyone who can read can easily understand it—two nights and one day, from late on Friday until early on Sunday.

Let those who can read understand.

Summary

The conclusions we have reached in this chapter are as follows. First, the disciples and followers of Yeshua not only believed they saw him alive after he had been dead and buried, but they actually did see him. Second, the resurrected Yeshua was as real as anyone you have ever seen, but he was Christ appearing as Yeshua. His body was not subject to the usual laws of physics, or nature, that rule over those of us still in the flesh. It was a spiritual body (*pneumatikon*), just as Paul relates in First Corinthians, a body capable of materializing inside a room with closed doors. Third, Yeshua was crucified on a Friday, and the Resurrection itself—whatever it may have comprised physically—took place sometime before dawn on the following Sunday (now celebrated as Easter). Fourth, apparently the Resurrection produced an image of the crucified Yeshua on the linen burial cloth in which he had been hastily wrapped late on the day of the crucifixion. This linen cloth was preserved as a precious religious object and is today known as the Shroud of Turin. Many say the Resurrection was God's stamp of approval on the person and work of Yeshua. Who are we to argue with that?

✝✝ *Deus Veritas Est* ✝✝

Chapter 7
The Way Things Are

WE ARE ABOUT TO RUSH IN WHERE ANGELS FEAR TO TREAD. The entire fabric of reality, in fact the very nature of the world—by which we mean the universe we inhabit—is not at all what you probably believe it to be. We humans live in a world we take for granted. We go about our business without a thought as to what we assume is real. Not infrequently, we even miss those things that are apparently real because we are so absorbed in ourselves. Wordsworth remarked, "The world is too much with us." He understated his case. When the authors lived in Las Cruces, New Mexico, a secretary giving us directions on how to find her doctor's office said to turn left on a certain street. To clarify, I asked her, "Toward the mountains?" She replied, "What mountains?" Now, several miles east of Las Cruces the magnificent Organ Mountains, with their imposing Organ Needles, rise nine thousand feet into the sky. They are an impressive presence as seen from anywhere within the city of Las Cruces. Yet this woman asked, "What mountains?"

The Beatles once wrote that it is "easy to go through life with eyes closed, misunderstanding all you see" ("Strawberry Fields Forever," by John Lennon and Paul McCartney, 1967). It is actually much worse than that. You cannot trust your eyes, or any of your other senses, to accurately depict this world.

Solid as a rock?

Doubtless you have heard the expression "as solid as the rock of Gibraltar." But just how solid is that rock? Here is a brief excerpt from an excellent book by Leonard Susskind, one of the leading theoretical physicists of our day:

> Take an ordinary brick. Its mass is roughly one kilogram. "Solid as a brick" is what we say. But bricks, solid as they seem, are almost entirely empty space. Put under enough pressure, they can be squeezed to a much smaller size. If the pressure were high enough, a brick could be squeezed to the size of a pinhead or even a virus. *And it would still be mostly empty space.* [Emphasis added]
>
> But there is a limit. I don't mean a practical limit based on the limitations of present-day technology. I am talking about laws of nature and fundamental physical principles. What is the smallest diameter that a one-kilogram object can occupy? The Planck size is an obvious guess, but it's not the right answer. [The] object can be squeezed until it becomes a black hole whose mass is one kilogram,* and no further: that's the smallest, most concentrated possible object with a given mass.
>
> Just what is the size of a one-kilogram black hole? The answer is probably smaller than you think. The Schwarzschild radius (radius of the horizon) of such a black hole is about one hundred million Planck lengths. That radius may sound big, but the truth is that it's a trillion times smaller than a single proton.
>
> —Susskind, Leonard, *The Black Hole War*. Page 369.
> New York: Little, Brown and Company, 2008

---

* There is a technical subtlety here. Squeezing a brick or other object increases its energy, and because of $E=mc^2$, it also increases its mass. But we can compensate for that in a variety of ways. What we want is to end up with the smallest possible one-kilogram object.

The brick-cum-black hole is so small that if you placed it next to a proton and then magnified them both until the black hole appeared to be the size of a proton, the proton next to it would swell to about the size of the state of New Jersey. And note Dr. Susskind's words: if you were to shrink a brick to the size of a virus it "would still be *mostly empty space.*"

If you could be shrunk to a size so small that the atoms in the brick looked to be the size of the solar system, and all of the atoms and molecules making up the brick could glow like stars, you would find those "stars" were much sparser than the stars in the nighttime sky (if you can still see the stars where you live!).

In other words, the entire universe we inhabit is mostly empty space. And that's not all there is to it, either.

There is nothing solid about *anything* in the universe. Particle physics has made enormous strides in the past century or so. Atoms, once thought to be the smallest building block of nature, turned out to have nuclei with tiny electrons orbiting around them. Atomic nuclei turned out to be made up of protons and neutrons clumped together. Further investigations showed that protons and neutrons were made up of still smaller particles called quarks (from James Joyce's *Finnegans Wake*, "Three quarks for Muster Mark!"). These strange critters come in six "flavors": up, down, strange, charm, bottom, and top. Believe us, you really don't want to know much more about them.

The most important thing about these "ultimate" particles is, however, that they are not really particles at all. They are tiny (putting it mildly) bundles of energy constrained to remain in one place—if undisturbed—rather than allowed to run loose like radiation such as light. Radiation, which is composed of other elementary "particles" called photons, travels at the speed of light. Like the bus in the 1994 movie *Speed*, a photon cannot slow down to less than the speed of light or it will cease to exist. Thus, there are two forms of energy in the universe: constrained energy, which we call particles, and unconstrained energy, which we call radiation. Both types can be called "wavicles," a word that means something with the properties of both a wave and a particle. These wavicles are now believed to be made up of little vibrating strings of energy; this is called string theory. It is in a state of evolution leading to who knows where.

As you may have suspected by this time, the relationship between constrained and unconstrained forms of energy is set by Einstein's famous equation $E = mc^2$, where E is the amount of energy contained in a wavicle, m is the mass [amount] of the wavicle, and c is the speed of light.

But the bottom line here is that there is nothing solid, nothing material, in this entire universe. **Nothing**.

This entire creation is only a vast illusion. A hoax. A chimera.

No wonder Yeshua asked how it profits a person to gain the world but lose his life. Gain *what*? In this world there is nothing real to gain.

The grand illusion

You may well be asking at this point: What is the point of creating what appears to be a glorious universe with rocks, oceans, planets, stars, and galaxies if there is really nothing there but a bunch of shimmering strings of energy? After all, if there is a Creator—and Yeshua among many others most emphatically insists that there is one—there must be some purpose in creating such a grand illusion. And indeed, there is one.

Those who arise to Christ consciousness see the true nature of the world. They see that the universe is not dead but a living thing—strings or no strings—and that all beings are connected with each other and with the world itself. This living universe Yeshua was wont to call the kingdom of God.

But why did God create the universe the way he did? How does it suit His purposes as the "best of all possible worlds" when obviously it is not the best of all possible worlds from our limited human viewpoint? Such questions have plagued human minds for millennia. The Hindus worked out much of this almost three thousand years ago. They call it the wonderful "Maya" of God. We human beings sweat and work our way through this mortal existence, and—at least commonly—without any concrete results to show for our efforts. What are the results of our existences, our lives in this world?

An intriguing science fiction movie came out in 2010 titled *Inception*. Its theme was the idea of a dream within a dream inside a dream. Without intending to, this film showed the key to the three levels of human consciousness. Our ordinary consciousness is but a dream. We do not realize we are dreaming. The dream is too real—the universe was designed to make this dream appear to be ultimate reality. It would not work were that not so. When we fall asleep and dream, we descend to the first level of consciousness, the simple level described earlier. We do not realize that we are dreaming and simply accept whatever happens as some kind of reality, which we do not question. On rare occasions some of us will realize that we are dreaming (this is called lucid dreaming). We then realize that the dream is not real and often will awaken. Sometimes this dream state is interrupted by what *Inception* called a "kicker." A kicker can be an external stimulus, such as a painful leg cramp or a loud noise. It can also be caused by dreaming that one has been killed. This will almost always awaken the dreamer, who then rises to the second level of consciousness: self awareness.

The awakened dreamer knows he is awake. He does not need to be told. But there is yet another level of consciousness: what we have called Christ consciousness. If one arises to the third level he sees that the world itself is an illusion and that he has awakened from a sort of dream—the dream of "reality." In the relatively few documented cases of Christ consciousness having come upon individuals, such as Yeshua or Buddha, this happens suddenly and without warning—like the lightning that flashes and lights up things from east to west. But just as there are "kickers" that awaken one from the first level of dreaming, there is a kicker that causes one to proceed to the next level: death. Just as dreaming being killed will awaken the dreamer, actually dying a physical death will "awaken" the reality-dreamer.

There is obviously a radical difference between dying and simply losing consciousness or falling asleep. But in a large number of cases persons have "died" on an operating table (or something similar) and experienced for a few minutes a curious state between life and death, a state which many have tried to describe with more or less success. Upon being resuscitated the subjects are suddenly "drawn back" to their bodies. These cases are widely known as "near-death experiences." We believe they are real.

All of this is very interesting, but it does not answer the root question: Why is the universe made this way?

The key to understanding the meaning of the world lies in the concept of inheritance. What can you take from this world to the next level of existence? Yeshua made it very clear that there is nothing you can do in this world that will profit you. There is nothing that you can take with you when you die. Jack Benny, a notorious miser, is said to have remarked, "If I can't take it with me I won't go." But we noticed that when the time came, he went—just like everyone else.

But there is one thing that you can take with you when you die. In fact, you *must* take it with you; you have no choice in the matter. And that is **who you are**.

Nothing that you do here in this life will ultimately matter except to you. You cannot do anyone else harm, even though it may seem that way to you. You can kill them—kill their mortal body—but you have no power over them. All you have accomplished by killing the other person is to promote them to the next level. But you have done yourself irreparable harm in the process.

ONE OF THE AUTHORS (David) once had a rather bizarre experience following an altercation with some lowlifes. One of the miscreants later confronted me and told me that he had a gun trained on me from the back of a van during the entire episode. I looked at him calmly and said, "You are lucky that you did not pull the trigger." He looked at me with amazement. "You mean *you* were lucky," he said. "No," I replied, "You were the one who was lucky. You would have done a terrible thing to yourself had you shot me." He just looked at me in stunned silence. I doubt that to this very day he understands what I meant.

The ultimate screen production

Like it or not, you are an actor in a gigantic movie production called "Life." William Shakespeare, himself a recipient of Christ consciousness (although Bucke believed he was really Roger Bacon), wrote: "All the world's a stage, And all the men and women merely players." [*As You Like It*, Act II, Scene VII] Much more recently the Beatles wrote, "Behind the shelter in the middle of the roundabout, A pretty nurse is selling poppies from a tray, And though she feels she's in a play, *she is anyway.*" ["Penny Lane," by John Lennon and Paul McCartney, 1967; emphasis added.] We are all actors in this huge cinematic production called *Life*. And like any film, once the filming is finished, all of the actors go home. Nobody is killed, no one is maimed, no harm is done. So it is with Life. The only difference is that "filming" is complete for each of us at the moment of our death. We don't go to our earthly home; we go to our Creator—we go on to the next level of Life.

But just like an earthly film, we are judged on how well we played our parts. Notice that in all the things that Yeshua says we should do or not do, his guiding principle is always the same: Treat others fairly; offer help when it is needed; do not lay up treasures on earth where "rust and moth consume" but rather lay up treasures in heaven for God, the Creator.

Those who are just and friendly make of themselves a sort of key, a key that fits in the doorway to the kingdom of God. This is why Yeshua said, "I am the way and the life. No one comes to the Father except by me." Christ is the lock, a lock that can only be opened by the key of an altruistic personality.

While it is true that the ultimate good of all beings is assured, there is no assurance that the way will be as easy for those who have evil in their hearts as for those who have goodness and mercy in their hearts. What may be in store for those who believe they have done evil things—things that did not actually happen at all in reality—we can only surmise. But from the few things Yeshua said of such persons, we may assume that they will have a rough time of things in the next level.

So the answer to the question "Why is the universe made this way?" is really quite simple. It is an immense school, a school for raising conscious beings. Like a sort of garden. And like any garden, some of what grows will be weeds, some more noxious than others, and some of what grows will bear fruit. Your mission, should you choose to accept it, is to be fruitful and not to become a weed in the garden of Life.

It is no accident that Yeshua picked the parable of the sower for one of his lessons to his disciples.

> The kingdom of God may be compared to a man who sowed good seed in his field; but while men were sleeping, his enemy came and sowed weeds among the wheat, and went away. So when the plants came up and bore grain, then the weeds appeared also. And the servants of the householder came and said to him, "Sir, did you not sow good seed in your field? How then has it weeds?" He said to them, "An enemy has done this." The servants said to him, "Then do you want us to go and gather them?" But he said, "No, lest in gathering the weeds you root up the wheat along with them. Let both grow together until the harvest; and at the harvest time I will tell the reapers, Gather the weeds first and bind them in bundles to be burned, but gather the wheat into my barn."
>
> —Mk 4:26-29; Mt 13:24-30

The parallels between this parable and what we have outlined in the preceding paragraphs should be obvious to anyone who is reading these words.

The problem of evil

Here we confront a problem that has vexed and confounded the great thinkers of the world since time immemorial. Great religious figures—saints, some of them—and philosophers, scholars and laypersons alike, all of them have tried to explain this conundrum: How can a God who is good and merciful allow evil to exist in a world that He created? To the best of our knowledge, no one has ever solved this problem. It has been discussed and argued by the best minds. Some have merely beat around the bush, so to speak, while yet others have attempted to explain it away. But no one has succeeded that we know of.

As we pointed out in Chapter Three, Emil Brunner (in *The Mediator*) states that the real damage of sin comprises the guilt that it engenders. What is done is done, and nothing we can do will ever erase the evil our sin has worked. The enormity of humanity's collective guilt requires no less than that the only begotten Son of God should suffer and die on the Cross to effect the Redemption. As Brunner correctly points out, this requires a unique once and for all event—the Revelation and Redemption through the Mediator—for its resolution. Note well the words "what is done is done." But is it?

The real nature of the universe as a vast illusion, a fake "reality" that is not real in the final analysis, argues against Brunner's position. If you were an actor making a movie and you "shot" another actor and "killed" him, would you feel guilty after the filming was over and the other fellow got up and dusted himself off? Or would you perhaps pat him on the back and say something like, "Good job of dying—it looked real to me."

The root problem here is that most of us do not realize we are only actors on the stage of Life. We think the things we see and do are real, permanent. What's done is done, right? No! It only appears to have been done. *In ultimate reality, nothing has been done.*

Many of us upon the "harvest" would probably say something like, "If only I'd known this was all some great charade, I would never have done some of the things I did." Brunner was right about the guilt that sin engenders; he was wrong to say that nothing we can do will ever erase the evil our sin has worked. There is no evil to erase. We cannot erase the guilt, however, especially when we see that the things we thought we gained by doing evil were illusory. They never existed. There was never anything to gain. When we thought we were "wasting" another person, we were really wasting ourselves.

The answer to the problem of evil is actually quite simple.

It does not exist—except in the minds of humans.

All evil is illusory, just like everything else in this universe. Only life, our being, is real. The rest is all a sideshow. It must be absolutely convincing, or it would not serve God's purpose in having created it in the first place. And we are positive that you, our reader, will agree that the world is a most convincing illusion.

Yet illusion it is.

It does not matter whether you believe this or not. Reality is its own justification, it does not depend upon the belief of anyone. *Wisdom is justified by all her children*.

But note this and note it well: There is one, and only one, aspect of evil that is real. That is in the mind of the person who does evil. That much is reality; the rest is all illusion. But to the extent that the people who think they have done evil believe that it is real, it is real to them and so it affects the nature of their character and being. You are what you believe you are. What others may think you are is irrelevant.

You, our readers, are living a life of illusion. The only thing that matters is what you make of yourselves. It does not matter what else you may do or not do.

And you cannot say you have not been warned.

Caveat pre-emptor!

～ ✿ ～

Note: We have been guilty in this work of treating the name and identity of God in a most cavalier manner. We do not know who or what God is; it is given to no person to know such things. Other than perhaps being viewed as the Life Force of the universe, God is not a thing to be apprehended by mere mortals. His name is merely a convenient placeholder for that which is beyond words.

Index

Index, continued

〜 ✿ 〜

A brief note to the so-called "politically correct"

Our readers may note the use of the personal pronouns "he," "him," and "his" in various places in the text of this work. Although we made some effort to avoid using these pronouns, there were places where they were virtually unavoidable. In these places we used the male pronouns in the sense that they were always used before: to relate to a person or persons of unknown gender. In the dictionary definition: "used in a generic sense or when the sex of the person is unspecified." We also made use of they, them, their wherever feasible. The use of constructions such as "he/she" or "he or she" are both unnecessary and verbose. Let no one be offended by these instances.

www.ingramcontent.com/pod-product-compliance
Lightning Source LLC
Chambersburg PA
CBHW060513030426
42337CB00015B/1871